Kids,
Classrooms,
& Contemporary
Education

PROBING THE HEADLINES
THAT IMPACT YOUR FAMILY

Don Closson

General Editor

kregel
PUBLICATIONS

Grand Rapids, MI 49501

Kids, Classrooms, & Contemporary Education: Probing the Headlines That Impact Your Family

Published by Kregel Publications, a division of Kregel, Inc., P.O. Box 2607, Grand Rapids, MI 49501. Kregel Publications provides trusted, biblical publications for Christian growth and service. Your comments and suggestions are valued.

For more information about Kregel Publications, visit our web site: www.kregel.com

Library of Congress Cataloging-in-Publication Data
Closson, Don.
    Kids, classrooms, & contemporary education: probing the headlines that impact your famliy / edited by Don Closson.
        p.   cm.
Includes bibliographical references.
    1. Church and education—United States.
2. Moral education—United States.
3. Education—Social aspects—United States.   I. Title.
LC368.C65   2000   306.43—dc 21   00-035726
                                                                            CIP
ISBN 0-8254-2034-2

Printed in the United States of America

1 2 3 4 5 / 04 03 02 01 00

Contents

Foreword

G. K. Chesterton wrote, "The point of having an open mind, like having an open mouth, is to close it on something solid." In this book Kerby Anderson, Don Closson, and Ray and Sue Bohlin display open minds on education and other contemporary issues, but they also show how to grab onto a biblical worldview and not let go.

Both openness and closure are vital in a culture committed to choice. We need to be open to the options currently afforded us, so that homeschooling can expand, school vouchers can have a fighting chance, addicts can enter faith-based anti-addiction programs instead of conventionally liberal ones, and creation can be taught alongside evolution. But we cannot agree to the notion that all options are equal.

The essays within are somewhat like homing pigeons in flight—they navigate many wind currents, but come back home (in this case, to the Bible) every time. From human cloning and welfare reform to multiculturalism and self-esteem curricula, these essays do not mimic the sun but the moon: Instead of trying to generate their own heat and light, they purposely reflect God's wisdom. Long ago, Augustine said, "If you believe in the gospel what you like, and reject what you don't like, it is not the gospel you believe, but yourself." This book is based on a belief in God.

—MARVIN OLASKY
Editor of *World* magazine and senior fellow,
Acton Institute

Contributors

Kerby Anderson is the president of Probe Ministries International. He received a B.S. from Oregon State University, an M.F.S. from Yale University, and an M.S. from Georgetown University. He is the author of several books, including *Genetic Engineering, Origin Science, Living Ethically in the 90s, Signs of Warning—Signs of Hope,* and *Moral Dilemmas.* He is a nationally syndicated columnist whose editorials have appeared in the *Dallas Morning News,* the *Miami Herald,* the *San Jose Mercury,* and the *Houston Post.* He is the host of the *Probe* radio program and frequently serves as guest host on *Point of View* (USA Radio Network) and *Open Line* (Moody Broadcasting Network).

Ray Bohlin is the executive director of Probe Ministries. He is a graduate of the University of Illinois (B.S., zoology), North Texas State University (M.S., population genetics), and the University of Texas at Dallas (M.S., Ph.D., molecular and cell biology). He is a co-author of the book *Natural Limits to Biological Change* and has published numerous journal articles. He was named a 1997–98 Research Fellow of the Discovery Institute's Center for the Renewal of Science and Culture.

Sue Bohlin is an associate speaker with Probe. She attended the University of Illinois and Trinity Evangelical Divinity School and has been a Bible teacher and Christian speaker for more than twenty years. In addition to being a professional calligrapher, she also manages Probe's web site.

Don Closson is the director of administration for Probe Ministries and is a vital part of Probe's research team. He received a B.S. in education from Southern Illinois University, an M.S. in educational administration from Illinois State University, and an M.S. (cum laude) in biblical studies from Dallas Theological Seminary. He served as a public school teacher and administrator before joining Probe Ministries in 1986 as a research associate in the field of education.

Part 1
Contemporary Issues

1

Abortion

Sue Bohlin

Abortion is one of the most divisive and controversial issues of our day. People generally have strong views about abortion. It is not a social issue of mere preference but an issue of life and death.

Abortion elicits clashes between two divergent worldviews. The humanistic worldview says, "Man is the highest standard. You don't answer to anyone, so do whatever you want." The Christian worldview, on the other hand, says, "We answer to God, and He has commanded us not to murder. We must always submit our desires and preferences to the authority of His Word."

The *real* reason we see such emotional, tenacious commitment to the availability of abortion goes even deeper than the issue of abortion: people want sexual freedom without consequences. Our culture has a definite agenda supporting any and all sexual expression. It's difficult to find a new movie, a successful television show, or a popular song that doesn't embrace this view of permissive sex. When the director of a crisis pregnancy center (CPC) in Dallas offered a school district a presentation supporting abstinence until marriage, the district turned her down. Their own presentation featured birth-control devices, and they couldn't let her talk about self-control one day if they were going to sell the kids on condoms the next day.

As a society, we are amazingly schizophrenic about this sort of thing. My son, who was born in 1982, is a *de facto* member of what they're calling the "Smoke-free Class of 2000." No one bats an eye at this worthy national goal of graduating an entire class of nonsmokers, but people laugh derisively at the thought of kids not having sex. Which is easier to get, a sex partner or a cigarette?

Teenagers are becoming more and more open about the fact that they are having sex, and this openness is a reflection of the sexual mores they see in movies and on TV and hear in music. The whole society is relaxing to the point that people who have chosen to remain chaste are openly ridiculed on television talk shows; the decision of a TV hero and role model for young people to lose his virginity is hailed as "responsible sex"; and an engaged man and woman who *don't* live together before their wedding are asked, "Why not?"

Western civilization has been heading down this path for a long time. With the rise of humanism during the Renaissance, societies began turning away from God's laws and God's ways. From the Enlightenment sprang a virtual worship of nature. Once nature, not God, became the standard for morality, people started believing that, because humans are a mere product of nature, anything we do naturally is normal and even good. Sex is natural, and sex is powerful, so it eventually followed that sexual expression was seen as a natural and normal part of all human existence in any circumstances, much on the level of eating and sleeping.

It's no coincidence that the two most heated issues of our day are abortion and homosexuality. Underlying both issues is an insistence on sexual freedom while thumbing one's nose at God and His laws.

Given the sexually charged atmosphere in which we live, it is not surprising that so many people are having sex outside of marriage and getting pregnant. Abortion is treated like an eraser; people see it as a way to rid themselves of the consequences of their sexual activity. Of course, there are always exceptions; pregnancies do occur as a result of incest and rape. Some women get pregnant because of someone else's sin. But does that make it right to kill the baby that has been conceived?

The Bible's View of the Unborn

Historically, hiding the evidence of sexual activity was the main reason for abortions. One of the early church fathers, Clement of Alexandria, maintained that "those who use abortifacient medicines to hide their fornication cause not only the outright murder of the fetus, but of the whole human race as well."[1]

Prochoice advocates don't like the use of the word *murder*. They maintain that no one really knows when human life begins, and they choose to believe that the idea of personhood at conception is a religious tenet and therefore invalid. It *is* a human life that is formed at conception. The zygote contains forty-six chromosomes, half contributed by each parent, in a unique configuration that has never before existed and never will again. It is not plant life or animal life, nor is it mere tissue like a tumor. From the moment of conception, the new life is genetically different from his or her mother, and it is not a part of her body like her tonsils or appendix. This new human being is a separate individual living inside the mother.

The Bible doesn't specifically address the subject of

abortion, probably because it is covered in the commandment "You shall not murder" (Exod. 20:13). But it does
give us insight into God's view of the unborn. In the Old
Testament, the Hebrew word for the unborn, *yeled,* is the
same word that is used for young children. The Hebrew
language did not have or need a separate word for preborn
babies. All children were children regardless of whether
they lived inside or outside the womb. In the New Testament, the same word is used to describe both the unborn
John the Baptist and the already-born baby Jesus. In the
Bible, the process of birth doesn't make any difference
concerning a baby's worth or status.

Psalm 139:13–16 gives us some wonderful insights
into God's intimate involvement in the development and
life of the pre-born infant.

> For you created my inmost being; you knit
> me together in my mother's womb. I praise
> you because I am fearfully and wonderfully
> made; your works are wonderful, I know
> that full well. My frame was not hidden
> from you when I was made in the secret
> place. When I was woven together in the
> depths of the earth, your eyes saw my un-
> formed body. All the days ordained for me
> were written in your book before one of
> them came to be.

All people, regardless of the circumstances of their
conception or whether they are healthy or handicapped,
have been personally knit together by God's fingers. He
has planned all of the days of the unborn child's life before
one of them has happened.

Sometimes you will hear a prochoice argument that the Bible does not put the same value on the life of the unborn as it puts on infants. Proponents of this view cite an Old Testament passage on personal injury law. Exodus 21:22–25 gives two penalties if fighting men hit a pregnant woman. The first penalty was a fine, and some people conclude from this that an unborn baby doesn't have the same value as a born child. But that penalty was for a situation in which nothing serious happened to the unborn child. If there *was* serious injury, the offender was severely punished with the same injury he inflicted. If either the mother or the baby died, the offender was to be put to death. This requirement actually shows very eloquently how valuable God considers the life of both the mother and her unborn baby.

Postabortion Syndrome

After having an abortion, many women feel a sense of relief at having avoided the stress and responsibility of pregnancy and a baby, but abortions eventually cause serious emotional damage in millions of women. The American Psychiatric Association has identified abortion as one of the stressor events that can trigger post-traumatic stress disorder (PTSD). Many of us associate PTSD with Vietnam veterans who are suffering from the effects of war, but postabortion syndrome (PAS) is a form of PTSD that affects women who have had abortions.

The death of a child is one of the biggest stress points a person can experience in life. PAS is the emotional stress of not grieving, not letting oneself feel the pain and suffering that is part of a loss. To be emotionally healthy, we all have to grieve through our losses; but what does a woman do when society tells her that there's nothing to grieve about? If a woman does not recognize her need to grieve for her baby, or if she does not allow the grieving to occur, that emotional pain will, nonetheless, go *somewhere.* Frequently, following an abortion, a woman goes into what one CPC counselor described as "self-destruct mode"— getting pregnant again, having an affair, punishing herself, and generally showing all of the variations of severe depression.

Depending on how stressed a woman is, PAS can surface within weeks or months of the abortion, or she can have a delayed reaction to it, typically seven to eight years later. Women experiencing PAS generally feel a confusing and overwhelming sense of guilt. One study reported that 92 percent of women who have had an abortion feel guilt.[2] One woman who is now involved in a postabortion healing group reports that after her abortion, the memory haunted her. She heard this little voice in her head: "Abortion, abortion; you're a terrible, awful person."[3] For many women, the guilt and shame is expressed through deep anger—at the doctors and abortion counselors for hurting her and her baby; at her husband, boyfriend, or parents for pressuring her into an abortion; and at herself for getting pregnant and having the abortion.

Many women who are dealing with the effects of abortion spend a great deal of emotional energy denying both the death of the baby and that what they did was wrong. A woman uses denial to keep herself from facing the fact that her child was killed and that she allowed it to happen. One young woman pleaded with my sister not to leave her alone the day she had an abortion. This hurting teen tried to keep her feelings at bay as she spent the afternoon telling dead-baby jokes.

Abortion is not an eraser to rub out a mistake or an

inconvenience. It has more than one victim; the woman and her baby are victims of abortion. It is essential that a woman grieve for her baby and face her role in the baby's death; in fact, women who allow themselves to grieve and understand their need to grieve are unlikely to experience PAS. But even more essential is the necessity for women who have had abortions to accept that there really has been a death, that abortion is sin, and that the Lord Jesus Christ's death covered *every* wrong that they have ever done. No sin—not even abortion—is greater than the power of His blood, and He offers total forgiveness and cleansing to everyone who will come to Him in faith.

The Sawyers' Story

Steve and Tessie Sawyer will never forget Halloween 1990. Tessie was four months pregnant, and her doctor had suggested, "Tess, you're thirty-five years old; let's do a neurological test on the baby. It's just a simple blood test." Sure, that was fine with Tessie . . . until the test results came back.

The alpha-fetoprotein test indicated that her blood count was extremely low. A normal count is 450, and hers was 120. This test has three parts, and the part that came back so abnormal tested for Down's syndrome. Neither Steve nor Tessie were the least bit prepared for the staggering news that something might be terribly wrong with their baby.

This baby was a surprise to the Sawyers, who already had two *very* active little boys and weren't anticipating any more. But, being believers, they knew that God's sense of humor and timing is something to be reckoned with.

Later, they did another alpha-fetoprotein test. Hoping against hope, they waited in anguish for the results to come back to Dallas from the laboratory in Santa Fe. But the second results were just as abnormal as the first. The doctor informed Steve and Tessie of their option to abort the baby because there was an almost certain indication that he would be handicapped. But they never considered abortion to be an option for them. The doctors wanted to do an amniocentesis test on Tess, but the Sawyers refused that, too.

At this point, the Sawyers' friends had two different perspectives. Their church friends were wonderfully supportive, both emotionally and in prayer; their unchurched friends questioned them: "Why don't you have an amnio?" Steve and Tessie were delighted, in the midst of their fear, to be able to share their faith that God was the One in control: "It doesn't matter what the test results would be. We're not aborting this baby. There's a risk of miscarriage or early labor with amniocentesis, and five months' peace of mind in exchange for our baby's life just isn't worth it."

At seven months, the doctor did a special, extensive sonogram. Down's syndrome babies have longer-than-normal extremities and unique facial features. But the doctor couldn't see anything unusual about the baby's bones, and he couldn't see the baby's face, either. The waiting and not knowing continued for two more months.

Tessie had a scheduled Caesarean section. As she was being prepped for surgery, the reality hit her that in a matter of moments their lives could be changed forever. That realization felt like a cold, hard iceball in her stomach. But Steve and Tessie were trusting God no matter what happened, believing in His love for them and their baby and that He was still in control.

The doctor delivered Lucas Clay Sawyer and looked him over. "He looks perfectly normal," he pronounced cautiously. But sometimes Down's syndrome takes a while to show up, and for the next twenty-four hours they ran a lot of tests on Luke. The Sawyers are glad to report that today he is the healthiest, most robust, smartest little kid you've ever seen.

All of the world's conventional wisdom advised Steve and Tessie, "Your baby is probably not normal. You should seriously consider abortion." But they are glad they didn't! We need to hear that test results are sometimes wrong. No one knows why the Sawyers' alpha-fetoprotein test came back with such dismal numbers on such a healthy baby. How many other healthy babies are being aborted after the parents get misleading or just plain wrong test results?

Handicapped Children

The Sawyers had a very happy ending to their story, but sometimes the tests do tell the truth, and babies really are sick or handicapped. There's no doubt about it; raising a handicapped child is painful and hard. Is it ever okay to abort a child whose life will be less than perfect?

We must ask ourselves, does the child deserve to die because of the handicap or illness? Life is hard, both for the handicapped person and for his or her parents. But it is significant that no organization of parents of children with mental or physical retardation has ever endorsed abortion.

Some people honestly believe that it's better to abort a handicapped child than to let him experience the difficult life ahead. Dr. C. Everett Koop, former Surgeon General of the United States, has performed thousands of pediatric surgeries on handicapped children. He remarks that disability and unhappiness do not necessarily go together. Some of the unhappiest children he has known had full mental and physical faculties whereas some of the happiest youngsters have borne very difficult burdens.[4] Life is more difficult for people with disabilities, but I can tell you personally that there is a precious side to it as well. I have lived most of my life with a physical handicap, but it hasn't stopped me from experiencing a fierce joy from living life to the fullest of the abilities I *do* have. I can honestly rejoice in my broken body because it is that very brokenness and weakness that makes it easier for others to see the power and glory of my Lord in me; His power is perfected in weakness.

Often, parents abort children with defects because they don't want to face the certain suffering and pain that comes with caring for a handicapped individual. By aborting the child, they believe that they are aborting the trouble. But as we discussed earlier, there is no way to avoid the consequences of abortion: the need to grieve, the guilt, the anger, and the depression are still there.

What if a baby is going to die anyway? Anencephalic babies, babies born without brains, have no hope of living any length of time. However, I think that we need to look at the larger picture, which includes God and His purposes for our lives. When a tragedy like this occurs, we can know that it is only happening because He has a reason behind it. God's will for us is not that we live easy lives but that we be changed into the image of Jesus. He wants us to be holy, not comfortable. The pain of difficult circumstances is often His chosen method to grow godliness both in us and in the lives of those touched by the tragedy of a child handicap. When it is a matter of life and death, as is abortion, it is not our place to avoid the pain.

My husband and I know what it is to bury a baby who

lived only nine days. We saw God use this situation to draw people to Himself and to teach, strengthen, and bless so many people beyond our immediate family. Despite the tremendous pain of that time, now that I have seen how God used it to glorify Himself, I would even go through it again.

Not all abortions are performed as a matter of convenience. Some are performed in very hard cases, such as a handicapped child or as the result of rape or incest. But again, we need to back off and look at things from an eternal perspective. God is the One who gives life, and only He has the right to take it away. Every person, born or unborn, is a precious soul made by God in His image. Every life is an entrustment from God that we need to celebrate and protect.

2

Christian Environmentalism

Ray Bohlin

T he news media are full of stories concerning environmental disasters of one kind or another, from global warming to endangered species, from destruction of the rain forests to nuclear accidents. But these environmental stories noticeably receive very little attention in Christian circles. So many other significant issues occupy our attention that we seem to think of the environment as someone else's problem. Many Christians are openly skeptical of the reality of any environmental crisis. They view the environment as a liberal issue, as New Age propaganda, or as just plain unimportant because this earth will be destroyed after the Millennium. What we fail to realize is that Christians have a sacred responsibility to the earth and the creatures inhabiting it. Humans are affecting the earth in an unprecedented manner, and we do not know what the short- or long-term effects will be.

The Seven Degradations of the Earth

Calvin DeWitt, in his book *The Environment and the Christian,* lists seven degradations of the earth.[1] First, land is being converted from wilderness to agricultural use and from agricultural use to urban areas at an ever-increasing rate. Some of these lands cannot be reclaimed, at least not in the near future.

Second, as many as three species a day become extinct. Once a species has disappeared, it is gone forever. Neither the species nor the role it occupied in the ecosystem can be retrieved.

Third, land continues to be degraded by the use of pesticides, herbicides, and fertilizers. Just because dichlorodiphenyltrichloroethane, better known simply as DDT, is no longer used does not mean that potentially harmful chemicals are not being used in its place.

Fourth, the treatment of hazardous chemicals and wastes continues as an unsolved problem. Hazardous chemicals seep into water sources from previously buried dumping grounds.

Fifth, pollution is rapidly becoming a global problem. Human garbage appears on the shores of uninhabited South Pacific islands, far from the shipping lanes, and DDT has been found in Antarctic penguins.

Sixth, our atmosphere appears to be changing. Is it warming as a result of the increase of gases such as carbon dioxide from the burning of fossil fuels? Is the ozone layer shrinking because of the use of chemicals contained in refrigerators, air conditioners, spray cans, and fire extinguishers? Although these questions cannot be answered easily, they must be asked.

Seventh, we are losing the experiences of cultures that have lived in harmony with the creation for hundreds or even thousands of years. Cultures such as the Mennonites and the Amish, as well as those of the rain forests, are crowded out by the expansion of civilization.

Never before have human beings wielded so much power over God's creation. Do we know what we are doing?

The Environmental Ethics of Naturalism and Pantheism

Some people have blamed Western culture's Judeo-Christian heritage for the environmental crisis. These critics point squarely at Genesis 1:26–28, where God commands His newest creation, humans, to have dominion over the earth and to rule and subdue it. This mandate is seen as a clear license to exploit the earth for humanity's own purposes. With this kind of philosophy, these critics ask, how can the earth ever be saved? Although I will deal with the inaccuracy of this interpretation a little later in this chapter, you can see why many of the leaders in the environmental movement are calling for a radical shift away from this Christian position. But what are the alternative worldviews?

The need to survive provides a rationale for environmental concern within an *evolutionary,* or *naturalistic, worldview.* Survival of the human species is the ultimate value. Humanity cannot continue to survive without a healthy planet. We must act to preserve the earth to insure the future of our children.

The evolutionary, or naturalistic, view of nature is, however, ultimately pragmatic. That is, nature has value only as long as we need it. The value of nature is contingent on the whim of egotistical people. If, as technology increases, we are able artificially to reproduce portions of the ecosystem for our survival needs, then certain aspects of nature lose their significance. We no longer need them to survive. This view is ultimately destructive because we will possess only that which we need. The rest of nature can be discarded.

Another alternative is the *pantheistic,* or *New Age, worldview.* Superficially, this view offers some hope. All of nature is equal because all is god and god is all. Nature is respected and valued because it is part of the essence of god. If humans have value, then nature has value.

But while pantheism elevates nature, it simultaneously degrades people and will ultimately degrade nature as well. To the pantheist, a person has no more value than a blade of grass. In India, with the blessings of the pantheists, the rats and cows spread disease and consume grain that humans need. To restrict the rats and cows would be to restrict god, so humans take second place to these animals. Humans are a part of nature; yet it is humans who are being restricted. Ultimately, *all* of nature is degraded.

Pantheism claims that what is, is right. To clean up the environment would mean eliminating the "undesirable" elements. But because god is all and in all, how can there be any undesirable elements? Pantheism fails because it makes no distinctions between people and nature.

The Christian Environmental Ethic

A true Christian environmental ethic differs from the naturalistic and the pantheistic ethics in that it is based on the reality of God as Creator and humanity as His image-bearer and steward.[2] God is the Creator of nature, not part of nature. He transcends nature (Gen. 1–2; Job 38–41; Pss. 19, 24, and 104; Rom. 1:18–20; Col. 1:16–17). All of nature, including humans, is equal in its origin. Nature has value in and of itself because God created it. Nature's value is intrinsic; it will not change because the fact of its creation will not change. The rock, the tree, and the cat deserve our respect because God made them to be as they are.

Although we are creatures and therefore are identified

with the other creatures, we are also created in God's image. This image is what separates us from the rest of creation (Gen. 1:26–27; Ps. 139:13–16). God did not bestow His image anywhere else in nature. Therefore, although a cat has value because God created it, it is inappropriate to romanticize the cat as though it had human emotions. All of God's creatures glorify Him by their very existence, but only one creature—humanity—is able to worship and serve Him by an act of the will.

Bearing the image of God carries a unique responsibility. We are called by God to rule and have dominion over the earth. In its proper sense, this calling means we are to be stewards or caretakers, not reckless exploiters. We are not sovereign over the lower orders of creation. Ownership is in the hands of the Lord.

God told Adam and Eve to cultivate and keep the garden (Gen. 2:15), and we may certainly use nature for our benefit, but we may use it only as God intends. Effective stewards understand that which they oversee, and science can help us discover the intricacies of nature. Technology puts the creation to use, but unnecessary waste and pollution degrades it and spoils the ability of creation to glorify its Creator. We are to exercise dominion over nature not as though we are entitled to exploit it but as though we are handling something borrowed or held in trust. In the parable of the talents in Matthew 25, the steward who merely buried his talent out of fear of losing it was severely chastised. What little he did have was taken away and given to him who already had a great deal. When Christ returns, His earth may well be handed back to Him rusted, corroded, polluted, and ugly. To what degree will you or I be held responsible?

Abuse of Dominion

Although God intended for us to live in harmony with nature, we have more often than not been at odds with nature. This reality tells us that we have not fulfilled our mandate. The source of our ecological crisis lies in our fallen nature and the abuse of our dominion. We are rebels who have set ourselves at the center of the universe. We have exploited created things as though they were nothing in themselves and as though we had an autonomous right to do so. Our abuse of our dominion becomes clear when we look at the value we place on time and money. Our often uncontrolled greed and haste have led to the deterioration of the environment. We evaluate projects almost exclusively in terms of their potential impact on humans. Let's look at residential development, for example.

Builders know that it is faster and more cost effective to bulldoze trees that are growing on the site of a proposed subdivision than it is to build the houses around them. Even if the uprooted trees are replaced with saplings once the houses are constructed, the loss of the mature trees enhances erosion; eliminates a means of absorbing pollutants, producing oxygen, and providing shade; and produces a scar that heals, if at all, slowly. Building around the trees, while more expensive and time-consuming, minimizes the destructive impact of human society on God's earth. But because of our sinful heart, the first option has been used more often than not.

Christians must treat nature as having value in itself, and we must be careful to exercise dominion without being destructive. The Bible contains numerous examples of the care with which we are expected to treat the environment. Leviticus 25:1–12 speaks of the care that Israel was to have for the land. Deuteronomy 25:4 and 22:6 indicate the proper care for domestic animals and a respect for wild-life. In Isaiah 5:8–10, the Lord judges those who have mis-used the land. Job 38:25–28 and Psalm 104:27–30 speak of God's nurture and care for His creation. And Jesus spoke on two occasions of how much the Father cared for even the smallest sparrow (Matt. 6:26; 10:29).

Christian Responsibility

Christians have a responsibility to the earth that ex-ceeds the responsibility of unredeemed people. We are the only ones who are rightly related to the Creator. We should be showing others the way to environmental responsibility.

Christians, of all people, should not be destroyers. We may cut down a tree to build a house or to make a fire but not just to cut it down. We have the right to rid our house of ants, but we should not forget to honor the ant in its right habitat. Although nothing is wrong with profit in the marketplace, in some cases we must voluntarily limit our profit to protect the environment.

When the church puts belief into practice, our human-ity and sense of beauty are restored. But this is not what is happening. Concern for the environment is not on the front burner of most evangelical Christians. The church has failed in its mission as steward of the earth. We have spoken out loudly against the materialism of science as expressed in the issues of abortion, human dignity, evolution, and genetic engineering, but we have shown ourselves to be little more than materialists in our technological orienta-tion toward nature.

By failing to fulfill our responsibilities to the earth, we are losing a great evangelistic opportunity. Many people in our society are seeking an improved environment, yet they think that most Christians don't care about ecological issues and that most churches offer no opportunity for involvement.

Because the environmental movement has been co-opted by those who are involved in the New Age movement, many Christians have begun to confuse interest in the environment with interest in pantheism and have hesitated to get involved. But we cannot allow the enemy to usurp leadership in an area that is rightfully ours. As the redeemed of the earth, our motivation to care for the land is even higher than that of the New Ager. Jesus has redeemed all of the effects of the curse, including our relationships with God, other people, and the creation (1 Cor. 15:21–22; Rom. 5:12–21). Although the heavens and the earth will eventually be destroyed and new ones will take their place, we should still work for healing now.

3

Human Cloning
Ray Bohlin

L ike so many other people, I was caught totally flat-footed and astonished by the announcement in February of 1997 of the successful cloning of the adult sheep Dolly. A few years ago I aired a radio program on the prospects of human cloning during which I considerably downplayed the possibilities. Earlier this year, we here at Probe had decided to rebroadcast this program because little had changed. When the announcement about Dolly was made, it was too late to pull the program from the schedule because tapes had already been sent to all of the radio stations, and there just wasn't time to replace or update the program. Consequently, I compiled into an article a few thoughts and comments on this historic breakthrough and quickly made it available on our web site to plug the gap temporarily.

Subsequently, the article was featured on Christian Leadership's web site, "Leadership University" (www.leaderu.com), and I started receiving numerous telephone calls and e-mails as a result. This chapter is now an updated and expanded version of that article to help us think through both the scientific and the moral implications of this stunning achievement.

Why Is Cloning So Difficult, and How Did They Do It?

The genetic material is the same in all cells of an organism (except the reproductive cells, sperm and egg, which have only half of the full complement of chromosomes). However, differentiated cells (liver cells, stomach cells, muscle cells, etc.) are biochemically programmed to perform limited functions, and all other functions are turned off. Most scientists felt that the reprogramming was next to impossible based on cloning attempts in frogs and mice.

So what did the scientists in Scotland do that was successful? Well, they took normal mammary cells from an adult ewe and starved them (i.e., denied them certain critical growth nutrients) to allow the cells to reach a dormant stage. This process of bringing the cells into dormancy apparently allows the cells' deoxyribonucleic acid (DNA) to be deprogrammed. Apparently, most, if not all, of the programming for specific functions of the mammary cells was turned off, and the DNA was made available for reprogramming. The starved mammary cells were then fused with an egg cell that had its nucleus removed. The egg cell was then stimulated to begin cell division by an electric pulse. Proteins already in the egg cell somehow altered the DNA from the mammary cell to be renewed for cell division and embryological functions.

As one might expect, the process was inefficient. Of 277 cell fusions, 29 began growing as embryos *in vitro* or in the petri dish. All 29 were implanted into 13 receptive ewes, yet only one became pregnant. As a result of these efforts, one lamb was born. This outcome translates to a success rate of only 3.4 percent, and the success rate is even less (0.36 percent) when one calculates using the 277 initial cell fusions attempted. In nature, on the other hand, somewhere between 33 and 50 percent of all fertilized eggs develop fully into newborns.[1]

Altogether, the procedure was rather nontechnical, and at this writing no one is really sure why it worked. The experiments continue. All earlier attempts to clone mice from adult cells failed. But clearly an astounding breakthrough has been made. We can be sure that numerous laboratories around the world will continue refining these experiments. The technique already is being tried with other mammalian species. Can this procedure be done with humans? Should we try it with humans? I'll deal with these questions later in this discussion.

Why Clone Anything?

Before proceeding to deal with the question of human cloning, a more basic concern must be addressed. Some people, for example, might be asking, "Why would anyone want to clone anything in the first place, but especially sheep?"

The purpose of these experiments was to find a more effective way to reproduce already genetically engineered sheep for production of pharmaceuticals. Sheep can be genetically engineered to produce a certain human protein or hormone in its milk. The human protein can then be harvested from the milk and sold on the market. This feat is accomplished by taking the human gene for the production of this protein or hormone and inserting it into an early sheep embryo. It is hoped that the embryo will grow into a sheep that will produce the protein.

This desired outcome is not a certainty, and although the process might improve, it will never be perfect. Mating the engineered sheep is also not foolproof because even mating with another genetically engineered sheep might result in lambs that have lost the inserted human gene and cannot produce the desired protein. Therefore, instead of trusting the somewhat unpredictable and time-consuming methods of normal animal husbandry to reproduce this genetic hybrid, cloning more directly assures that the engineered gene product will not be lost.

Cloning technology might offer other benefits. Reprogramming the nucleus of other cells, such as nerve cells, could lead to procedures to stimulate degenerating nerve cells to be replaced by newly growing nerve cells. Nerve cells in adults do not ordinarily regenerate or reproduce. This potential benefit could have important implications for people who suffer from Parkinson's disease and Alzheimer's disease.

If the process can actually be perfected to the extent that production costs are reduced and the quality of the eventual product is improved, this result would be a legitimate research goal. The simplicity of the technique, although still inefficient, makes this goal plausible. But other questions must be answered.

One critical question concerns the lifespan of Dolly. All cells have a built-in senescence, or death, after so many cell divisions. Dolly began as a cell from a ewe that was already six years old. A normal lifespan for a ewe is about eleven years. Will Dolly live to see her seventh birthday? Actually, most cell divisions are used up during embryological development. Dolly's cells might disappear even earlier. This possibility is critical because a ten-year-old sheep is considered elderly, and lambing and wool production decline in sheep after their seventh year. My guess is that because Dolly's genes were reprogrammed from mammary cell functions to embryological functions, the senescence clock was also reset to the beginning. I expect Dolly to live a normal lifespan.

Whether Dolly would be reproductively fertile was also uncertain. Frogs cloned from tadpole cells are usually sterile. A possibility was that although Dolly is normal anatomically, the cloning process might somehow interfere with the proper development of the reproductive cells. If this were the case, there might have been other problems not immediately detectable. This question has now been answered since Dolly has birthed three normal lambs over the last two years.

Can We Clone Humans?

Although we have established that animal cloning might be permissible and even scientifically useful, what about human cloning? First, is it feasible? Second, just because we can do it, should we? Should we even try?

At this point, it is reasonable to assume that because the procedure works with sheep and possibly with cattle (the experiments with cattle are already under way), it should also work with humans. This does not mean, however, that there might not be unique barriers to cloning humans as opposed to cloning sheep.

Some authorities suggest that by using the particular procedure developed by the researchers in Scotland, sheep might be easier to clone because sheep embryos do not employ the DNA in the nucleus until after three to four cell divisions. This fact might give the egg cell sufficient time to reprogram the DNA from mammary cell functions to egg cell functions. Human and mouse cells employ the nuclear DNA after only the second cell division. This fact might be why similar experiments have not worked in mice. Therefore, human cells and mouse cells might not be capable of being cloned because of this difference.

If this barrier does indeed exist, it is not necessarily insurmountable. The news of a cloned sheep was surprising enough that no one, including me, is now going to step out on the same sawed-off limb and predict that it can't eventually work with humans. I mentioned earlier that the procedure is so startlingly nontechnical that numerous laboratories around the world could immediately begin their own cloning research programs with a minimum of investment and expertise. Although I fully expect that many laboratories will begin studies on cloning mammalian species besides sheep, I'm not so sure about cloning of humans.

In 1993, researchers in the United States employed well-known techniques to artificially duplicate human embryos. They immediately became embroiled in a firestorm of public scrutiny that they did not anticipate nor enjoy. Even other researchers in the field criticized them for jumping ahead without scrutinizing the ethical ramifications. The public reaction was no doubt very sobering to the rest of the scientific community. Many countries either have completely banned experimentation in human cloning or at least have imposed a temporary moratorium so that the ethical questions can be properly investigated before stepping ahead. Even the researchers in Scotland who were responsible for Dolly have plainly stated that they see no reason to pursue human cloning and are personally repulsed by the idea.

Some people in the scientific community, however, think that the ability to do something is reason enough to do it. In this case, I believe that they are the minority. For example, in the 1970s, when genetic technology was first being developed, molecular biologists imposed a moratorium of their own until critical questions could be answered. Also, although nuclear weapons have been produced for more than fifty years, only two of them have been used, and that was fifty-two years ago. Many such weapons are now being dismantled. These cases show us that human restraint, though rare, is possible.

Although it is reasonable to believe that humans can be cloned and that someone somewhere might try to do so, the overall climate is so against it that I don't think we will see it announced anytime soon.

Why Clone Humans?

Overall, the public reaction toward cloning human beings has been negative, and this reaction is rather curious in a culture that is admittedly post-Christian in orientation. Nevertheless, many people still want to draw a distinction between animals and humans.

As Christians, we understand this desire because we assert that humans are made in the image of God whereas animals are not. There is, therefore, a clear demarcation between animals and humans. But in an evolutionary view, humans are nothing special—just another animal species. Tom Siegfried offered the expected reaction in an editorial titled "It's hard to see a reason why a human Dolly is evil," which appeared in the *Dallas Morning News*.[2] He summarized his perspective thus: "The ability to clone is part of gaining deeper knowledge of life itself. So Dolly should not be seen as scary, but as a signal that life still conceals many miracles for humans to discover." To the naturalist, any knowledge is valuable, and the means to obtain it is justified essentially by its benefit to society.

With this view in mind, let's explore some of the reasons

people have suggested that human cloning is a worth-while proposition and deal with some of the questions people are asking.

Concerns About Human Cloning

Much can be learned about human embryonic development by researching human cloning. Although this statement is true, it is precisely the reasoning that Nazi Germany used to justify experimentation on Jews. The Nazis conducted experiments on exposure to cold, water, and other extreme conditions using human subjects, frequently to the point of death, because data on human subjects were deemed indispensable. Of course, we know now that animal models work just as well; consequently, there is no need to use human models to gain these data.

Will humans be cloned for spare parts? A few writers have suggested that some individuals might want to establish an embryonic clone to be frozen and stored. Then, in the event of a childhood disease that requires a transplant, the embryo can be thawed, implanted into a surrogate, and raised to a sufficient age for the spare organ to be harvested and transplanted. Although this feat is certainly possible, I consider it very unlikely that such practices would be sanctioned by any government because it completely tosses aside the uniqueness of humanity and trashes the concept of human dignity. That doesn't mean, however, that someone won't try it.

Will human cloning be used to replace a dying infant or child? This use is certainly a possibility, but we must ask if taking such a course of action is an appropriate way to deal with loss. Unrealistic expectations might be placed on a clone that would not be placed on a normally produced child. The cloned child might be the same genetically but different in other respects, a situation that could create more frustration than comfort.

Will humans be cloned to provide children for otherwise childless couples? This possibility is the reason most often given for human cloning, yet the argument is unpersuasive when there are already so many children awaiting adoption. Also, it devalues children to the level of a commodity. And if *in vitro* fertilization seems expensive at five thousand to eight thousand dollars a try, cloning will be more so.

Will human clones have souls? In my mind, they will be no different than an identical twin or a baby that results from *in vitro* fertilization. How a single fertilized egg splits in two to become two individuals is a similar mystery, but it happens.

Does cloning threaten genetic diversity? Excessive cloning might indeed deplete the genetic diversity of an animal population, leaving the population susceptible to disease and other disasters. But most biologists are aware of these problems, and I would not expect this to be a major concern unless cloning were the only means available to continue a species.

If the technique is perfected in animals first, will this save the tragic loss of fetal life that resulted from the early human experimentation with in vitro *fertilization?* In vitro fertilization was perfected in humans before scientists knew how effective the procedure would be. This resulted in many destroyed human lives in the embryonic stages. The success rate is still only 10 to 20 percent. The success rate of normal fertilization and implantation is about 33 to 50 percent. Although animal models will help, unique aspects to human development will exist that can be known and overcome only by direct human experimentation that does not respect the sanctity of human life.

Cloning provides a means for lesbians to have children as a couple. One lesbian would supply the nucleus, and the other one would provide the egg. The egg does contain some unique genetic material in the mitochondria that are not contributed by sperm or nucleus. The individual cells from each partner are fused to create a new individual, although all of the nuclear genetic material comes from only one cell. The real question is whether this is the proper environment in which to raise children. Homosexual "marriages" are not really marriages in the normal understanding of the term, and the technological hoops through which one must jump for any gay couple to have children should be a clear warning that something is wrong with the whole arrangement.

Are human clones unique individuals? Even identical twins manage to forge their own identities. The same would be true of clones. In fact, this point may argue strongly against the usefulness of cloning because we can never reproduce all of the life experiences that have molded a particular personality. The genes will be the same, but the environment and the spirit will be different.

On the whole, I find the prospect of animal cloning potentially useful. But I wonder if the procedure is as perfectible as some people hope. It might end up being an inefficient process to achieve the desired result. Human cloning is fraught with too many possible difficulties, from the waste of human fetal life during research and development to the commercializing of human babies, with far too little potential advantage to individuals and society. What is to be learned about embryonic development through cloning experiments can be learned through animal experimentation. The cloning of adult human beings is an unnecessary and unethical practice that should be strongly discouraged if not banned altogether.

4

Stairway to Heaven

Materialism and the Church

Don Closson

O ne of the most popular rock songs of the 1970s begins with the lyrics, "There's a lady who's sure all that glitters is gold, and she's buying a stairway to heaven." The words, written by Jimmy Page, Robert Plant, and John Paul Jones of the group Led Zeppelin, reflect the fashionable message of antimaterialism that pervaded much of rock music in the late 1960s and 1970s. The notion of dropping out of the rat race and rejecting the corporate mentality of one's parents formed the foundation of many rock musicians' careers.

Today, one often hears people refer to the entire decade of the 1980s as the "me decade," as if during that period Americans were somehow more self-centered and money hungry than during any other previous period. One popular newspaper framed that mind-set with the following poem:

> Now I lay me down to sleep
> I pray my Cuisinart to keep
> I pray my stocks are on the rise
> And that my analyst is wise
> That all the wine I sip is white

> And that my hot tub is watertight
> That racquetball won't get too tough
> That all my sushi's fresh enough
> I pray my cordless phone still works
> That my career won't lose its perqs
> My microwave won't radiate
> My condo won't depreciate
> I pray my health club doesn't close
> And that my money market grows
> If I go broke before I wake
> I pray my Volvo they won't take.[1]

Christianity has had a much longer tradition of critiquing a materialistic lifestyle. Jesus' life was lived as a rejection of the merely material perspective. In His Sermon on the Mount, Jesus tells us that we can become enslaved by the desire for money and things. He pleads with us to go beyond concerns for what we will consume and to seek our Creator and His will. In Matthew 6:24–25, Jesus taught, "No one can serve two masters. Either he will hate the one and love the other, or he will be devoted to the one and despise the other. You cannot serve both God and Money. Therefore I tell you, do not worry about your life, what you will eat or drink; or about your body, what you will wear. Is not life more important than food, and the body more important than clothes?"

In spite of the fact that large segments of both popular and religious culture apparently hold materialism in low regard, surveys indicate that it influences the thinking of many Americans. In a recent survey, George Barna found that 72 percent of Americans believe that people are blessed by God so that they can enjoy life as much as possible, and 58 percent agree with the statement that the primary purpose of life is enjoyment and fulfillment. Eighty-one percent believe that God helps those who help themselves.[2]

These responses point to the validity of what has been called our "therapeutic culture." The first commandment of this culture is "Do whatever makes you feel good, whatever helps you to cope materially." When Jesus was asked what was the most important commandment, He responded by saying that we are to love God (not things) with all of our heart, soul, mind, and strength and to love our neighbors as ourselves (Mark 12:30–31). That kind of love is self-denying and sacrificial.

The Millionaire and the Dreamer

In his book *The Gospel and the American Dream,* Bruce Shelley tells the true story of a man who boasted to others that he would be a millionaire by age thirty-five. This young man was known as a really nice guy who had a good sense of humor. People considered him to be bright, thoughtful, and generous to a fault. In 1984, he had acquired many of the appearances of success. He was flying to Dallas from Phoenix weekly on business. He drove a nice company car and had moved his family into an exclusive neighborhood. He was also doing all of the things that wealthy young men should do. He was the program chairman of the local Lions Club, president of the two hundred-member Arizona chapter of the American Institute of Chemical Engineers, and a board member for the local Boys Club. However, on a Sunday in May 1985, the family missed church for the first time in months. The aspiring millionaire spent the day struggling in vain to scrape together enough cash to salvage his business, his image, and his pride. At 11:30 that night, after the family went to bed, he laid out his insurance policies and then went into the garage. He got into his expensive, company-provided BMW and turned on the ignition. He was dead within minutes.

A friend of mine had an important job working for a large defense contractor in the Dallas area. After a number of years, he had placed a substantial amount of money into 401(k)s and other investments, money that most people would consider their financial security for their retirement years. But he also had completed a master's degree in theology and then left his well-paying job to teach part time at a local Christian college for far less pay. However, this young man's real dream was to purchase a large old house in the city and fill it with students who desired to know God deeply and to live in community with others who wanted to do the same. Eventually, he found just such a house. Knowing that it would consume most, if not all, of his savings, he bought it.

Now, a few years down the road, my friend has virtually run out of money. But his dream is coming true. The house has been completely renovated, and both graduate and undergraduate students are living in it. He conducts Bible studies and reading groups with both students living in the house and some who do not. He is broke, but he is excited and rejoicing in what God is doing.

The two lives I've described depict two different faith systems. The millionaire, claiming to have faith in the God of the Bible, ultimately had placed his faith in things. When he was in danger of losing them, he gave up on life itself. My friend who is renovating the old house is just about out of money. However, he is optimistic and excited about the ministry he is having in the lives of the students who live there. He is aware of the financial difficulties that his dream presents, but he is trusting in God to provide even when good business sense might argue against it.

Could it be that many Christians have succumbed to the notion of rugged individualism, placing the building of an earthly empire above the building of God's kingdom? James 5:1–3 holds a severe warning for those tempted by wealth: "Now listen, you rich people, weep and wail because of the misery that is coming upon you. . . ." God warns believers against placing their faith in things and treating people as expendable commodities.

The Sources of Materialism

To understand the grasp materialism has on so many people, including Christians, we have to understand the sources of materialism. I propose that there are two kinds of materialism: philosophical materialism and functional materialism.

C. S. Lewis defined philosophical materialism as the belief held by people who "think that matter and space just happen to exist, and always have existed, nobody knows why; and that the matter, behaving in certain fixed ways, has just happened, by a sort of fluke, to produce creatures like ourselves who are able to think."[3] Philosophical materialism imagines a universe without a spiritual dimension. Carl Sagan, one of the most popular and prolific science writers in history, held to philosophical materialism. He wrote that the physical cosmos is all that exists, and we inhabit this cosmos as the result of a series of chance occurrences.

If one holds to this position, being anything but materialistic would be illogical. This does not mean that philosophical materialists treat all people as if they were merely things. It just means that they have no good reason for treating them in any other way. The atheist philosopher Kai Nielsen wrote, "We have not been able to show that reason requires the moral point of view, or that all really rational persons, unhoodwinked by myth or ideology, need not be individual egoists or classical amoralists. . . . Pure practical reason, even with a good knowledge of the facts, will not take you to morality."[4] Bertrand Russell wrote that humans are nothing more than impure lumps of carbon and water, and yet late in life he talked about his love for humanity.[5] What is there to love about impure lumps of carbon and water? It is hard to live out philosophical materialism. That is why very few people hold to this viewpoint.

Survey after survey reveals that the vast majority of Americans believe that God exists. If most Americans believe in God, why do so many of them live as though He is unimportant? Why do they act like functional materialists? Why do so many Christians measure their success in life by materialistic standards? We could blame our modern society. The triumph of scientism, the tendency to reduce every phenomenon to materialistic components, often leaves little room for behavior motivated by a spiritual reality. However, I believe that the problem goes deeper.

Every believer experiences a battle between the spirit and the flesh. In Galatians 5:17, Paul writes, "For the sinful nature desires what is contrary to the Spirit, and the Spirit what is contrary to the sinful nature. They are in conflict with each other, so that you do not do what you want." Further, he warns the Galatians that people whose lives are filled with selfish ambition and envy, among other things, will not inherit the kingdom of God. This is not to say that one will lose one's salvation, but that a life consumed by materialistic desires is probably devoid of a spiritual dimension altogether. If the Holy Spirit is not evident, there is no regeneration and no salvation.

Jesus' ministry was filled with teachings about materialism, both in parables and more directly. In fact, the beginning of His ministry is highlighted by His experience in the wilderness, where Satan tempted Him with materialistic seduction. Consideration of the temptation of Christ sheds light on how our surrounding culture operates in much the same way as Satan did in the desert.

Materialistic Temptations

In examining the seduction of materialism and its impact on the church, it is significant that at the beginning of Jesus' short ministry the Spirit led Him into the wilderness to experience deprivation and temptation (Matt. 4:1). Biblical writers often used the word *tempt* to mean "to try something for the purpose of demonstrating its worth or faithfulness."[6] Jesus' fasting in the desert provides His followers with an example of earthly suffering with which they could relate. It also provides a model for how to resist temptation.

Satan's testing of Jesus in Matthew 4 should be a warning for Christians in our highly materialistic culture. Satan still uses these techniques today to test the faithfulness of the body of Christ. Matthew tells us that the first temptation by Satan preyed on Jesus' basic bodily needs. Jesus was hungry; He had fasted for forty days and nights. Satan suggested that He turn the stones into bread, something well within Jesus' capabilities. Believers wrestle with the same suggestion from Satan today. But what is wrong with fulfilling normal bodily functions? We need food, clothing, and shelter (and some would add sex) to survive. God made us that way, right?

Satan's temptation is to reduce human nature to what might be called the *will-to-pleasure* principle, the idea that sensual pleasure explains all of our motivations and needs. Jesus responded with the Scripture, "It is written: 'Man does not live on bread alone, but on every word that comes from the mouth of God'" (Matt. 4:4). He replaced the *will-to-pleasure* view of human nature with a *will-to-meaning* view. We cannot live on food alone; humans must have meaning and purpose to survive.

In his personal struggle to survive a Nazi concentration camp, psychologist Victor Frankl discovered that when men lost meaning or hope, they quickly died.[7] Humankind needs a transcendent reason to continue striving against the struggles of life. It is the Word of God that provides the only true foundation for this struggle.

Next, Jesus was tempted with a formula for *instant status*. Satan suggested that He perform a miracle that would surely convince the Jews that He is their Messiah. He should throw Himself down from the temple. His survival would be just the right sign necessary for the Jews to recognize Him. The only problem with this plan was that it was not the will of the Father. Jesus might gain notoriety, but He would lose His integrity. Jesus responded by declaring that we are not to put God to the test. We are not to presume that God will accept our plans with miraculous support. We conform to His will; He does not conform to ours.

Finally, Satan showed Jesus all of the kingdoms of the world and told Him that they were His if He would only worship him. Satan was tempting Jesus with what might be called the *success syndrome*. If Jesus' goal was to be the king of the Jews, why not do it the easy way? Jesus replied to him, "Away from me, Satan! For it is written: 'Worship the Lord your God, and serve him only'" (Matt 4:10). Like-wise, we are not called to success but to obedience. There are many messages in our surrounding culture that encourage the pleasure principle, the importance of status, and the idea of success at all costs. However, as believers, we are to seek a higher standard than pleasure, regardless of what others think, and often in the face of disappointing results.

Material Possessions and the Church

A Cuban pastor recently attended a conference in Dallas and noticed how people here often say that they have no time. He said that people in Cuba have relatively few things but rarely run out of time. This brings to mind the idea of opportunity cost. This rule from economics tells us that if we spend our resources on one thing, we cannot use them on another thing. If our focus is on things and our time is spent buying, using, fixing, and replacing them, do we really have time to build the relationships with people necessary to communicate the gospel?[8]

In his book *A Biblical Theology of Material Possessions,* Dr. Gene Getz suggests some biblical principles to guide Christians in their relationship to material things.[9] First, he notes biblical warnings against being materialistic. As we mentioned earlier, it is possible for believers to be in bondage to things; we cannot serve both things and God. Second, accumulating wealth brings with it specific temptations. The fifth chapter of James and the book of Amos describe how financial power can lead to economic injustice and other forms of oppression. In Acts 8, Luke warns believers that some people in the church will use the Christian message to benefit themselves financially. Because this danger was present at the very beginning of the church, we should not be surprised or discouraged when we see it happen today.

As the church looks for the imminent return of Christ, believers should avoid the increasing tendency to intensify love for self, money, and pleasure. The warning in 2 Timothy 3 is to avoid those who succumb to this temptation. Christians also have to be on constant guard against self-deception and rationalization when living in an affluent society. When the church at Laodicea imagined itself self-sufficient and without need, Jesus described them as wretched, pitiful, poor, blind, and naked (Rev. 3:17–18).

How, then, do Christians avoid materialism? The apostle Paul writes that godliness with contentment is great gain (1 Tim. 6:6). Do we have enough faith to believe this revealed truth? If so, our first priority in life should be the pursuit of contentment rather than riches. As Paul declares, "I have learned the secret of being content in any and every situation, whether well fed or hungry, whether living in plenty or in want" (Phil. 4:12b).

When God blesses us with abundance, our goal should be to use it creatively to further God's kingdom, for where our treasure is so is our heart (Matt. 6:19–21). Jesus taught the disciples not to be absorbed with worry about the future but to seek His kingdom and His righteousness (Matt. 6:34).

What happens when people use their material possessions in harmony with God's will? Acts 2 gives a good example of the results. When believers had given up their claim to even their personal belongings, God added to their number daily. How we use our wealth has a great impact on the watching world. A second result was that love and unity were created in the body of Christ. When the church members were sharing their personal possessions, "all the believers were one in heart and mind"(Acts 4:32).

What could be more powerful in our materialistic age than a church using its wealth to further God's kingdom, unite in love, and grow daily in numbers? This is how the early church had such a remarkable impact on its surrounding culture. Do we have enough faith to trust God for the same results today?

5

Violence in Society

Kerby Anderson

Growing up used to be less traumatic just a few decades ago. Children back then worried about such things as a flat tire on their Schwinn and hoped that their teacher wouldn't give too much homework.

How life has changed! In a 1994 poll, more than half of the children questioned said that they were afraid of violent crime against them or a family member.[1] Are these kids just paranoid, or is there a real problem?

No, this is not an irrational fear based upon a false perception of danger. Life has indeed become more violent and more dangerous for children. Consider the following statistics: One in six youths between the ages of ten and seventeen has seen or knows someone who has been shot.[2] The estimated number of child abuse victims increased 40 percent between 1985 and 1991.[3] Children under eighteen were 244 percent more likely to be killed by guns in 1993 than they were in 1986.[4] Violent crime has increased by more than 560 percent since 1960.[5]

The innocence of childhood has been replaced by the very real threat of violence. Kids in school try to avoid fights in the hall, walk home in fear, and sometimes sleep in bathtubs to protect themselves from stray bullets fired during drive-by shootings.

Even families living in "safe" neighborhoods are concerned. They might feel safe today, but they are always reminded that violence can intrude at any moment. Polly Klaas and her family no doubt felt safe in Petaluma, California. But on October 1, 1993, Polly was abducted from her suburban home during a sleepover with two friends. If she can be abducted and murdered, so can nearly any other child.

A child's exposure to violence is pervasive. Children see violence in their schools, neighborhoods, and homes. The daily news is rife with reports of child molestations and abductions. Wars in foreign lands and daily reports of murder, rape, and robberies also heighten a child's perception of potential violence.

Television in the home is the greatest source of visual violence for children. The average child watches eight thousand televised murders and one hundred thousand acts of violence before finishing elementary school. That number more than doubles by the time he or she reaches age eighteen.[6]

The latest scourge is music television (MTV). Teenagers listen to more than ten thousand hours of rock music, and this impact is intensified as they spend countless hours in front of MTV, watching violent and sensual images that go far beyond the images shown on commercial television.

It's a scary world, and children are exposed to more violence than any generation in recent memory. An article in *Newsweek* magazine concluded, "It gets dark early in the Midwest this time of year. Long before many parents are home from work, the shadows creep up the walls and gather in the corners, while on the carpet a little figure sprawls in the glow emanating from an anchorman's tan. There's been a murder in the Loop, a fire in a nightclub, an indictment of another priest. Red and white lights swirl in urgent pinwheels as the ambulances howl down the dark streets. And one more crime that never gets reported, because there's no one to arrest. Who killed childhood? We all did."[7]

Violence and Human Nature

Violence has always been a part of the human condition because of our sin nature (Rom. 3:23). But modern families are exposed to even more violence than previous generations were because of the media. Any night of the week, the average viewer can see levels of violence approaching and even exceeding the Roman gladiatorial games.

Does this exposure have an effect? Certainly it does. The Bible teaches that "as a man thinks in his heart, so is he" (Prov. 23:7 NKJV). What we view and what we think about affects our actions.

Defenders of television programs say that isn't true. They contend that televised imagery makes people neither violent nor callous to suffering. But if televised imagery doesn't affect human behavior, then the TV networks should refund billions of advertising dollars to TV sponsors.

In essence, TV executives are talking out of both sides of their mouths. On the one side, they try to convince advertisers that a thirty-second commercial can influence consumer behavior. On the other side, they deny that a one-hour program wrapped around the commercials can influence social behavior.

So, how violent are the media, and what impact do the media have on members of our family? First, we will look at violence in the movies and on television. Then we'll consider the impact of violence on our families.

Ezra Pound once said that artists are "the antennae of the race." If that is so, then we are, judging by the latest fare of violence in the movies, a very sick society. The body count is staggering: thirty-two people are killed in *RoboCop,* and eighty-one people are killed in the sequel. In *Die Hard* 2, 264 people are killed. The film *Silence of the Lambs* deals with a psychopath who murders women and skins them.

Who would have imagined just a few years ago that the top grossing films would be replete with blood, gore, and violence? No wonder some film critics now say that the most violent place on earth is the Hollywood set.

Violence has always been a part of movie-making, but, until recently, really violent movies were seen by only the fringe of mass culture. Violence has now gone mainstream. Bloody films are being watched by people other than just punk rockers. Family station wagons and vans pull up to movie theaters showing R-rated slasher films. And middle America watches these same programs a few months later on cable TV or on video. Many of the movies seen at home wouldn't have been shown in theaters ten to twenty years ago.

Movie violence today is louder, bloodier, and more anatomically precise than ever before. When a bad guy was shot in a black-and-white Western, the most we saw was a puff of smoke and a few drops of fake blood. Now the sights, sounds, and special effects often jar us more than the real thing. Slow motion, pyrotechnics, and a penchant for leaving nothing to the imagination conspire to make movies and TV shows more gruesome than ever.

Children, especially, confront an increasingly violent

world with few limits. As concerned parents and citizens, we must do what we can to reduce the level of violence in our society through discernment and wise public policy. We need to set limits both in our homes and in the community.

Media Violence and Human Behavior

Children's greatest exposure to violence comes from television. TV shows, movies edited for television, and video games expose young children to a level of violence unimaginable just a few years ago. The violent content of television includes more than just the twenty-two-minute programs produced by the networks. At a very young age, children are seeing a level of violence and mayhem that in the past might have been seen only by a few police officers and military personnel. TV brings hitting, kicking, stabbing, shooting, and dismemberment right into homes daily.

The impact on behavior is predictable. Two prominent surgeon generals' reports in the last two decades link violence on television and aggressive behavior in children and teenagers. In addition, the National Institute of Mental Health issued a ninety-four-page report, *Television and Behavior: Ten Years of Scientific Progress and Implications for the Eighties*. They found "overwhelming" scientific evidence that "excessive" violence on television spills over into the playground and the streets.[8] In one five-year study of 732 children, "several kinds of aggression—conflicts with parents, fighting and delinquency—were all positively correlated with the total amount of television viewing."[9]

Long-term studies are even more disturbing. University of Illinois psychologist Leonard Eron studied children first at age eight and then again at age eighteen. He found that television habits established at the age of eight influenced aggressive behavior throughout childhood and adolescent years. The more violent the programs preferred by boys in the third grade, the more aggressive their behavior, both at that time and ten years later. He therefore concluded that "the effect of television violence on aggression is cumulative."[10]

Twenty years later, Eron and Rowell Huesmann found that the pattern had continued. He and his researchers found that children who watched significant amounts of TV violence at the age of eight were consistently more likely to commit violent crimes or engage in child or spousal abuse at thirty.[11] They concluded "that heavy exposure to televised violence is one of the causes of aggressive behavior, crime and violence in society. Television violence affects youngsters of all ages, of both genders, at all socioeconomic levels and all levels of intelligence."[12]

Since the Huesmanns' report in the 1980s, MTV has come on the scene with even more troubling images. Adolescents already listen to an estimated 10,500 hours of rock music between the seventh and twelfth grades. Now they also spend countless hours in front of MTV, seeing the visual images of rock songs that depict violence, rebellion, sadomasochism, the occult, drug abuse, and promiscuity. MTV reaches fifty-seven million cable households, and its video images are even more lurid than the ones shown on regular TV.[13] Music videos filled with sex, rape, murder, and other images of mayhem assault the senses. And MTV cartoons such as *Beavis and Butt-Head* assault the sensibilities while enticing young people to start fires and commit other acts of violence.[14] Critics count an average of eighteen acts of violence during each hour of MTV videos.[15]

Violent images on television and in the movies do contribute to greater violence in society. Both sociological studies and common sense dictate that we do something to reduce the violence in the media before it further damages society.

Violence and Heavy Viewers

Confronted with such statistics as we've cited, many parents respond that their children aren't allowed to watch violent programs. Such action is commendable, but some of the greatest dangers of television are more subtle and insidious. It now appears that simply watching television for long periods can manipulate one's worldview—regardless of whether the content is particularly violent.

George Gerbner and Larry Gross, working at the Annenberg School of Communications in the 1970s, found that heavy viewers of TV live in a scary world. "We have found that people who watch a lot of TV see the real world as more dangerous and frightening than those who watch very little. Heavy viewers are less trustful of their fellow citizens, and more fearful of the real world."[16]

So heavy viewers were less trustful and more fearful than the average citizen. But what constitutes a heavy viewer? Gerber and Gross defined *heavy viewers* as "adults who watch an average of four or more hours of television a day." Approximately one-third of all American adults fit that category.

They found that violence on prime-time TV exaggerated heavy viewers' fears about the threat of danger in the real world. Heavy viewers, for example, were less likely to trust someone than were light viewers. Heavy viewers also tended to overestimate the likelihood of their being involved in a violent crime.

If this is true of *adults,* imagine how much TV violence affects *children's* perception of the world. Gerbner and Gross say, "Imagine spending six hours a day at the local movie house when you were twelve years old. No parent would have permitted it. Yet, in our sample of children, nearly half the twelve-year-olds watch an average of six or more hours of television per day." This would mean that a large portion of young people fit into the category of heavy viewers. Their view of the world must be profoundly shaped by TV. Gerbner and Gross therefore conclude, "If adults can be so accepting of the reality of television, imagine its effect on children. By the time the average American child reaches public school, he has already spent several years in an electronic nursery school."[17]

Television violence subtly affects both adults and children. Although we might not personally feel or observe the effects of TV violence, we should not ignore the growing body of data that suggest that televised imagery does affect our perception and behavior. Obviously, something must be done. Parents, programmers, and general citizens must take responsible actions to prevent the increasing violence in our society. Violence in homes, violence on television, violence in the movies, and violence in the schools contribute to the increasingly violent society in which we live. We have a responsibility to make a difference and apply the appropriate principles to help stem the tide of violence in our society.

Suggestions for Dealing with Violence in the Media

Christians must address this issue of violence in our society. Following are a number of specific suggestions for dealing with violence.

1. Learn about the impact of violence in our society. Share this material with your pastor, elders, deacons, and other church members. Help them understand how important this issue is to them and their community.

2. Create a safe environment. Families live in the midst of violence. We must make our homes safe for our families. A child should feel that his or her world is safe. Providing care and protection are obvious first steps, but parents must also establish limits, provide emotional security, and teach values and virtue in the home.

3. Parents should limit the amount of media exposure in their homes. The average young person sees entirely too much violence on TV and at the movies. Set limits to what a child watches, and evaluate both the quantity and the quality of their media input (Rom. 12:2). Focus on what is pure, beautiful, true, right, honorable, excellent, and praiseworthy (Phil. 4:8).

4. Watch TV with your children. Obviously, we should limit the amount of TV our children watch. But when they watch television, we should try to watch it with them. We can encourage discussion with children during the programs. The plots and actions of the programs provide a natural context for discussion and teach important principles about relationships and violence. The discussion could focus on how cartoon characters or TV actors could solve their problems without resorting to violence. TV often ignores the consequences of violence. What are the consequences in real life?

5. Develop children's faith and trust in God. Children at an early age instinctively trust their parents. As the children grow, parents should work to develop their child's trust in God. God is sovereign and omnipotent. Children should learn to trust Him in their lives and depend upon Him to watch over them and keep them safe.

6. Discuss the reasons for pain and suffering in the world. We live in a fallen world (Genesis 3), and even those who follow God will encounter pain, suffering, and violence. Bad things do happen to good people.

7. Teach vigilance without hysteria. By talking about the dangers in society, some parents have instilled fear—even terror—in their children. We need to balance our discussions with them and not make them hysterical. Kids have been known to become hysterical if a car comes down their street or if someone looks at them.

8. Work to establish broadcaster guidelines. No TV or movie producer wants to unilaterally disarm all of the actors on their screens out of fear that viewers will watch other programs and movies. Yet many of these same TV and movie producers would like to tone down the violence, but they don't want to be the first to do so. National standards would be able to achieve what individuals would not do by themselves in a competitive market.

Violence is the scourge of our society, but we can make a difference. We must educate ourselves about its influence and impact on our lives. Please feel free to write or call Probe Ministries for more information on this topic. And then take time to apply the principles developed here to make a difference in your home and community. You can help stem the tide of violence in our society.

6

Teen Drug Abuse

Kerby Anderson

A Nine Inch Nails album, *The Downward Spiral,* features a song titled "My Self Destruct" with the following lyrics: "I am the needle in your vein and I control you, I am the high you can't sustain and I control you." Another song, titled "Hurt," explores drugs as a means of escape: "The needle tears a hole, the old familiar sting, try to kill it all away."

Five Dodge City, Kansas, teenagers, high on marijuana, killed a stranger for no apparent reason. Three West Palm Beach, Florida, teenagers mixed beer, rum, marijuana, and cocaine. They then kidnapped and set ablaze a tourist from Brooklyn.

Nearly everywhere we look, the consequences of drug abuse can be seen. Violent street gangs, family violence, train crashes, the spread of AIDS, and babies born with cocaine dependency testify to the pervasive influence of drugs in our world.

The statistics are staggering. The average age of first alcohol use is twelve, and the average age of first drug use is thirteen. According to the National Institute on Drug Abuse, 93 percent of all teenagers have some experience with alcohol by the end of their senior year of high school and 6 percent drink daily. Almost two-thirds of all American young people try illicit drugs before they finish high school. One out of sixteen seniors smokes marijuana daily, and 20 percent have done so for at least a month sometime in their lives.[1] A recent poll found that adolescents listed drugs as the most important problem facing people their age, followed by crime and violence in school and social pressures.[2]

Drugs have changed the social landscape of America. Street gangs spring up nearly overnight looking for the enormous financial profits that drugs can bring. Organized crime is also involved in setting up franchises that would make McDonald's envious. But these are not hamburgers. In the world of drugs, homicidally vicious gangs compete for market share with murderous results. Many gang members outgun the police with their weapons of choice: semiautomatic pistols, AK-47s, and Uzis. Drug dealers have also gone high tech, using cellular phones and computers to keep track of deals while their teenage runners wear phone beepers in school.

The Parents' Resource Institute for Drug Education (PRIDE) reports that children who abuse illicit drugs are significantly more likely to carry a gun to school, take part in gang activities, think of suicide, threaten harm to others, and get in trouble with the police than children who abstain.

One survey released by the University of Colorado shows that the problem of drug use is not just outside the church. The study involved nearly fourteen thousand junior high and high school youth and compared churched young people with unchurched young people. It found very little difference between the two groups. For example, 88 percent of the unchurched young people reported drinking beer as compared to 80 percent of churched young people. When asked how many had tried marijuana, 47 percent of the unchurched young people had done so compared to 38 percent of the churched youth. For amphetamines and barbiturates, 28 percent of the unchurched had tried them while 22 percent of the churched young people had tried them. And for cocaine use, the percentage was 14 percent for unchurched youths and 11 percent for churched youths.[3]

Fighting drug use often seems futile. When drug dealers are arrested, they are often released prematurely because court dockets are overloaded. Plea bargaining and paroles are standard fare as the revolving doors of justice spin faster. As the casualties mount in this war against drugs, some commentators have begun to suggest that the best solution is to legalize drugs. But you don't win a war by surrendering. If drugs were legalized, addiction would increase, as would health costs, and government would once again capitulate to societal pressures and shirk its responsibility to establish moral law.

If legalization is not the answer, then something must be done about the abuse of drugs such as alcohol, cocaine, marijuana, heroin, and PCP. The National Center for Health Statistics estimated the annual medical cost of drug abuse to be nearly 60 billion dollars, and the annual medical bill for alcohol abuse was nearly 100 billion dollars.

How to Fight the Drug Battle

Society must fight America's drug epidemic on five major fronts. The first battlefront is *at the border.* Federal agents must patrol the 8,426 miles of deeply indented Florida coastline and the 2,067 mile border with Mexico. This task is formidable, but vast distances are not the only problem.

The smugglers they are seeking have almost unlimited funds and some of the best equipment available. Fortunately, the federal interdiction forces (namely, U.S. Customs, the U.S. Drug Enforcement Administration, and the Immigration and Naturalization Service) are improving their capability. Customs forces have been increased, and all three agencies are getting more sophisticated equipment.

The second battlefront is *law enforcement at home.* Police must crack down by making more arrests, gaining more convictions that result in longer sentences, and seizing more of the drug dealers' assets. Unfortunately, law enforcement successes pale in comparison to the volume of drug traffic. Even the most effective crackdowns seem to do little more than move drugs from one location to another.

An effective weapon on this battlefront is a 1984 law that makes it easier to seize the assets of drug dealers before their conviction. In some cities, police have even confiscated the cars of suburbanites who drive into the city to buy crack.

Attempts to deter drug dealing, however, have been limited by flaws in the criminal justice system. A lack of jail cells prevents significant prosecution of drug dealers. Even if this problem were alleviated, the shortage of judges would still result in the quick release of drug pushers.

A third battlefront is *drug testing.* Many government and business organizations are implementing routine testing to reduce the demand for drugs. The theory is simple: Drug testing is a greater deterrent to drug use than the remote possibility of going to jail. People who know that they will have to pass a urine test to get a job are going to be much less likely to dabble in drugs. In 1980, 27 percent of some twenty thousand military personnel admitted to using drugs in the previous thirty days. Five years later, when drug testing was implemented, the proportion dropped to 9 percent.[4]

But drug testing is not without its opponents. Civil libertarians think that this deterrent is not worth the resulting loss of personal privacy. Some unions believe that random testing in the workplace would violate the Fourth Amendment's prohibition against unreasonable searches.

A fourth battleground is *drug treatment.* Drug addicts need help, but the major issue is who should provide the treatment and who should foot the bill. Private hospital programs are now a 4 billion-dollars-a-year business with a daily cost of as much as five hundred dollars per bed per day. This cost is clearly out of reach for many addicts who do not have employers or insurance companies who can pick up the costs.

A fifth battleground is *education.* Teaching children the dangers of drugs can be an important step in helping them learn to say no to drugs. The National Institute on Drug Abuse estimates that 72 percent of the nation's elementary and secondary school children are receiving some kind of drug education.[5]

Should We Legalize Drugs?

Those who are weary of the war on drugs have suggested that we should decriminalize drugs. Former Surgeon General Joycelyn Elders suggested that we study the impact of legalizing drugs. For years, an alliance of liberals and libertarians have promoted the idea that legalizing drugs would reduce drug costs and drug crimes in this country. But would it? Let's look at some of the arguments for drug legalization.

1. *Legalization will take the profit out of the drug business.*

As surprising as it might sound, relatively few drug dealers actually earn huge sums of money. Most people in the crack business are low-level runners who make very little money. Many crack dealers smoke more crack than they sell. The drug cartels are the ones making the big profits.

Would legalizing drugs really affect large drug dealers or drug cartels in any appreciable way? Drug cartels would still control prices and supplies even if drugs were legalized in this country. If government set the price for legalized drugs, criminals could undercut the price and supply whatever the government did not supply.

Addicts would not be significantly affected by legalization. Does anyone seriously believe that their behavior would change just because they are now using legal drugs instead of illegal drugs? They would still use theft and prostitution to support their habits.

Proponents of legalization also argue that legalizing drugs would reduce the cost of drugs and thus reduce the supply of drugs flowing into this country. Recent history, however, suggests that just the opposite would take place. When cocaine first hit the United States, it was expensive and difficult to obtain. But when more of it was dumped into this country and made readily available in less-expensive vials of crack, both drug addiction and drug-related crimes rose.

2. *Drug legalization will reduce drug use.* Proponents argue that legalizing drugs will make them less appealing because they will no longer be "forbidden fruit." However, logic and social statistics suggest that decriminalizing drugs will actually increase drug use.

Those who argue for the legalization of drugs often point to Prohibition as a failed social experiment. But was it? When Prohibition was in effect, alcohol consumption declined by 30 to 50 percent, and death from cirrhosis of the liver fell dramatically.[6] One study found that suicides and drug-related arrests also declined by 50 percent.[7] After the repeal of the Eighteenth Amendment in 1933, alcoholism rose. So did alcohol-related crimes and accidents. If anything, Prohibition proves the point that decriminalization would increase drug use.

Comparing alcohol and drugs actually strengthens the argument against legalization because many drugs are even more addictive than alcohol. Consider, for example, the difference between alcohol and cocaine. Alcohol has an addiction rate of approximately 10 percent, whereas cocaine has an addiction rate as high as 75 percent.[8]

Many drugs are actually "gateway drugs" to other drugs. A 1992 article in *The Journal of Primary Prevention* reported that marijuana use is essentially a "necessary" condition for the occurrence of cocaine use. Other research shows that involvement with illicit drugs is a developmental phenomenon, age correlates with use, and cigarette and alcohol use precede marijuana use.[9]

Robert DuPont, former head of the National Institute on Drug Abuse, argues that the potential market for legal drugs can be compared to the number who use alcohol (140 million persons). If his analysis is correct, then approximately 50 million Americans would eventually use legal cocaine.

Great Britain's experiment with drug legalization has been a disaster. Between 1960 and 1970, the number of British heroin addicts increased thirtyfold. During the 1980s, it increased by as much as 40 percent per year. By contrast, the number of heroin addicts in the United States fifteen years ago (one-half million) is the same number we have today.

But the real question is not whether alcohol or drugs is worse. The question is whether we can accept both legalized alcohol and legalized drugs. Legalized alcohol currently leads to one hundred thousand deaths a year and costs us 99 billion dollars a year.[10] We don't need to legalize drugs, too.

3. *Legalization will reduce social costs.* "We are losing the war on drugs," say drug legalization proponents, "so let's cut the costs of drug enforcement by decriminalizing drugs."

The United States now spends 11 billion dollars a year to combat drug-related crime. If drugs were legalized, some crime-fighting costs might drop, but many social costs would certainly increase: an increase in other forms of crime (to support habits), the costs of drug-related accidents, and higher welfare costs.

Statistics from states that have decriminalized marijuana demonstrate the validity of this concern. In California, within the first six months of decriminalization, arrests for driving under the influence of drugs rose 46 percent for adults and 71.4 percent for juveniles.[11] The use of marijuana doubled in Alaska and Oregon when it was decriminalized in those states.[12]

Crime would certainly increase. Justice Department figures show that approximately one-third of inmates used drugs before they committed their crimes. Juvenile crime would no doubt increase as well. A 1990 study published in the *Journal of Drug Issues* found a strong association between the severity of the crime and the type of substance used; the more intoxicating the substance, the more serious the incident.[13]

Meanwhile, both worker productivity and student productivity would decrease. The Drug Enforcement Administration estimates that drug decriminalization would cost society more than alcohol and tobacco combined, perhaps as much as 140 to 210 billion dollars a year in lost productivity and job-related accidents alone.[14]

Government services would no doubt have to be expanded to pay for additional drug education and treatment for those who are addicted to legal drugs. Child protective services would no doubt have to expand to deal with resulting child abuse. Patrick Murphy, a court-appointed lawyer for thirty-one thousand abused and neglected children in Chicago, says that more than 80 percent of the cases of physical and sexual abuse of children now involve drugs. Legalizing drugs will not reduce these crimes; it would only make the problem worse.[15]

Is it accurate to say that we are losing the war on drugs? Drug use in this country was on the decline in the 1980s as a result of a strong antidrug campaign. The number of casual cocaine users, for example, dropped from 12 million in 1985 to 6 million in 1991. You don't win a war by surrendering. Legalizing drugs in this country would constitute surrender in the drug war at a time when we have substantial evidence that we can win this battle on a number of fronts.

4. *Government should not dictate moral policy on drugs.* Libertarians who promote drug legalization value personal freedom. They believe that government should not dictate morals and fear that our civil liberties will be threatened by a tougher policy against drugs.

The true threat to our freedoms, however, comes from the foreign drug cartels, drug lords in this country, and drug dealers on our streets. Legalizing drugs would send the wrong message to society. Those who are involved in drug use eventually see that drugs ultimately lead to prison or death, so they begin to seek help.

Obviously, some people are going to use drugs whether they are legal or illegal. Keeping drugs illegal maintains criminal sanctions that persuade most people that their lives are best lived without drugs. Legalization, on the other hand, removes the incentive to stay away from drugs and thereby increases drug use.

William Bennett said, "I didn't have to become a drug czar to be opposed to legalized marijuana. As Secretary of Education, I realized that, given the state of American education, the last thing we needed was a policy that made widely available a substance that impairs memory, concentration, and attention span. Why in God's name foster the use of a drug that makes you stupid?"[16]

A Biblical Perspective

Some people might believe that the Bible has little to say about drugs, but this is not so. First, the Bible has a great deal to say about the most common and most abused drug: alcohol. Ephesians 5:18 admonishes Christians not to be drunk with wine. In many places in Scripture drunkenness is called a sin (Deut. 21:20–21; Amos 6:1; 1 Cor. 6:9–10; Gal. 5:19–20). In Proverbs 20:1, Isaiah 5:11, and Habakkuk 2:15–16, the Bible also warns of the dangers of drinking alcohol. If the Bible warns of the danger of alcohol, then by implication it is also warning of the dangers of taking other kinds of drugs.

Second, drugs were an integral part of many ancient Near Eastern societies. For example, the pagan cultures surrounding the nation of Israel used drugs as part of their religious ceremonies. Both the Old Testament and the New Testament condemn sorcery and witchcraft. The word translated *sorcery* comes from the Greek word from which we get the English words *pharmacy* and *pharmaceutical.* In ancient times, drugs were prepared by a witch or shaman.

Drugs were used to enter into the spiritual world by inducing an altered state of consciousness that allowed demons to take over the user's mind. In that day, drug use was tied to sorcery. In our day, many people use drugs merely for "recreational" purposes, but we cannot discount the occult connection.

Galatians 5:19–21 says, "The acts of the sinful nature are obvious: sexual immorality, impurity and debauchery; idolatry and witchcraft [which includes the use of drugs]; hatred, discord, jealousy, fits of rage, selfish ambition, dissensions, factions, and envy; drunkenness, orgies, and the like. I warn you, as I did before, that those who live like this will not inherit the kingdom of God." The word *witchcraft* here is also translated *sorcery* and refers to the use of drugs. The apostle Paul calls witchcraft that was associated with drug use a sin. The nonmedical use of drugs is considered one of the acts of the sinful nature. Drug use, whether to "get a high" or to tap into the occult, is one of the acts of the sinful nature whereby users demonstrate their depraved and carnal nature.

The psychic effects of drugs should not be discounted. A questionnaire designed by Charles Tate and sent to known users of marijuana documented some disturbing findings. In his article in *Psychology Today,* he noted that one-fourth of the marijuana users who responded to his questionnaire reported that they were taken over and controlled by an evil person or power during their drug-induced experience. Also, more than half of those questioned said that they have experienced religious or "spiritual" sensations in which they meet spiritual beings.[17]

Many proponents of the drug culture have linked drug use to spiritual values. During the 1960s, Timothy Leary and Alan Watts referred to the "religious" and "mystical" experience gained through the use of LSD (along with other drugs) as a prime reason for taking drugs.[18]

No doubt, drugs are dangerous not only to our body but also to our spirit. As Christians, we must warn our children and our society of the dangers of drugs.

7

United Nations Conferences

Kerby Anderson

A lthough United Nations (UN) conferences have been taking place frequently over the last two decades, most Americans have ignored the proceedings and their ominous implications. Recent conferences in Cairo, Beijing, and Istanbul have been vivid reminders of the radical ideology of the UN and the threat it poses to our faith, families, and freedom.

The direction of the last few conferences illustrates this point. The 1992 Earth Summit in Rio de Janeiro established an environmental foundation for all of the United Nation's radical social and economic agendas. The 1994 Cairo Conference focused on population control and pushed abortion and contraception as solutions to the perceived "problem" of overpopulation. The 1995 Women's Conference in Beijing, China, proved to be the most radical of the conferences. It continued to push abortion as a human right and attempted to make sexual orientation a human right by promoting the idea that genders are not clearly defined but are socially constructed. The White House already has created an Inter-Agency Council to implement the Beijing platform in the private sector and in every executive agency.

These conferences culminated in the conference known as Habitat II, which was held in Istanbul, Turkey, and built upon the foundation of the other conferences. Wally N'Dow, Secretary General of Habitat II, predicts that the conference will be a "new beginning that will reflect and implement the actions called for at the unprecedented continuum of global conferences that have marked this closing decade of the century." He said that "a new global social contract for building sustainable human settlements must be forged" for the "new global urban world order." Mindful of the controversy surrounding the other conferences, he declared, "There will be no roll-back of any of the conferences, including Beijing."[1]

Habitat II focused on the problems of urban centers. Its goal is to create "economically, socially and environmentally thriving urban communities" to better the lives of people living in Third World countries. Although the goals are commendable, the agenda of the conference participants went far beyond urban blight.

A key concept in the Habitat II agenda is sustainable development. In the school curriculum developed by the United Nations, *sustainable development* is defined as "meeting the needs of the present generation without damaging the Earth's resources in such a way that would prevent future generations from meeting [their needs]."[2] It includes "changing wasteful consumption patterns" and "emphasizing equitable development" to "bridge the gap between rich and poor countries." In practice, sustainable development is a radical concept that will limit the amount of food, energy, or general resources that citizens of a nation can consume. Rather than consuming what they can afford, "rich" nations (such as the United States) might be allowed to consume only what they need to stay alive.

One UN publication declares that we "must learn to live differently" and calls for this international agency to "ensure that the benefits of development are distributed equally." To achieve this so-called "equal distribution," there must be a redistribution of wealth throughout the planet. The United Nations has already drafted specific plans for implementing sustainable development in the United States. In spite of the frightening implications of these conferences, U.S. taxpayers have been footing the bill for them and their radical agendas.

Habitat II: Global Taxes and National Sovereignty

The conference in Istanbul, Turkey, is illustrative of another major concern, namely, the threat that these conferences pose to our national sovereignty.

Habitat II called for national governments to manage economic systems, including public and private investment practices, consumption patterns, and public policy. UN Secretary General Boutros Boutros Ghali told the first plenary session that he wanted the conference to be a "Conference of Partners."

Another section was devoted to the international community and its involvement with national governments. The Global Plan of Action calls for the international community to force changes in the world's economic structures.

The United Nations also intends to reach sustainable development by changing the structure of national governments. In fact, the Habitat II agenda depends upon UN oversight of national, regional, state, and local governments. The document asks city administrators to redesign their regulations, political systems, and judicial and legislative procedures. It was no accident that the conference was filled with mayors from many U.S. cities as well as from cities around the world.

The Habitat II document proposed that "government at all levels should encourage . . . walking, cycling, and public transport . . . through appropriate pricing . . . and regulatory measures."[3] Governments are charged with the responsibility of encouraging citizens to walk, ride bicycles, or take public transportation. This would be accomplished by the heavy taxation and burdensome regulations often found in socialist economies.

UN Secretary General Boutros Boutros Ghali also has called for global taxes to fund the United Nations. During the conference, the United States was harshly criticized for being delinquent in its payments to the United Nations. It currently owes 1.5 billion dollars and pays about 25 percent of the UN budget and nearly 40 percent of the "peacekeeping" costs. The United Nations hopes to implement these global taxes in the next few years so it can be free of U.S. influence and enact its radical global agenda.

The global taxes that Boutros Boutros Ghali proposed would be received from international currency transactions, energy shipments, and international travel. If implemented, they would remove the United Nations' dependence on sovereign nations. No longer would the United States or other countries have a check and balance against an international organization. The United Nations could pay for its activities, fund its peacekeeping forces, and conduct many of its affairs independently of the United States.

Canadian developer Maurice Strong is often considered a likely candidate to become the future Secretary General of the United Nations. He has called for a shift in our current thinking. He has stated that this change in thinking "will require a vast strengthening of the multilateral system, including the United Nations. . . . We must now forge a new Earth Ethic which will inspire all people and nations to join in a new global partnership of North, South, East and West."[4]

This global vision should especially concern Christians who are mindful of end-times prophecy. At a time when the world seems to be moving swiftly toward global government, the prospect of a stronger United Nations autonomous of sovereign nations is a scary scenario. This bolder and stronger United Nations would further erode U.S. sovereignty and strengthen the hand of world leaders who are promoting globalist visions of a one-world government.

UN Conferences: Four Areas of Concern

The ideologies from recent UN conferences are influencing several areas of life that Christians should be concerned about.

The first area is *education.* Many of the concepts from Habitat II, such as "sustainable development," have already infiltrated America's schools. Textbooks promote global citizenship and minimize national sovereignty. Other textbooks blame rich countries (such as the United States) for retarding the growth and development of poorer countries. "Tolerance" and "global peace" are emphasized as the ultimate aims of society. The federal Goals 2000 program for education in this country provides the perfect mechanism to transmit these global UN philosophies into school curricula.

A second area is the *impact on families.* The Habitat II conference continued the UN attempt to redefine the family. Many UN leaders see the traditional family as an obstacle to UN dominance.

The Habitat II platform stated that "in different cultural, political and social systems, various forms of the family exist." Many participants asked that "sexual orientation" be included as a civil rights category. In many ways, this request merely extended the concept promoted during the Beijing Women's Conference that gender be defined not as male and female but as one of five genders that are socially constructed. Habitat II also promoted "gendered cities" that are to be organized in terms of "gender roles."

The third area has to do with *population.* The UN Population Fund says that population growth is a key inhibitor of sustainable growth. UN recommendations of population control are based upon the faulty premise that the world is in the midst of a population explosion that cannot be sustained. Participants raised the fear of losing resources even though empirical evidence points to the contrary.

Because of the United Nations' antipopulation bias, the Habitat II document emphasizes "sustainable development" as the mechanism for population control. Thus, "family planning" is a key concept, and the document therefore emphasizes surgical abortions and chemical abortions (e.g., RU-486). The Habitat platform specifically mentions "reproductive health services" for women in human settlements and calls for government management of economic and population growth.

A final area of concern is *ecology and pollution.* At the 1992 UN Earth Summit, Strong stated, "It is clear that current lifestyles and consumption of large amounts of frozen convenience foods, use of fossil fuels, appliances, home and workplace air conditioners and suburban housing are not sustainable."[5] Because Strong will probably succeed Boutros Ghali as UN Secretary General, people are rightly concerned about his New Age views on ecology.

The Habitat II document encourages nations to use heavy taxation and various regulations to ensure that citizens walk, ride bicycles, and take public transportation.

The threats posed by these UN conferences are real. American citizens must fight these radical ideas and ensure that our politicians do not give away our sovereignty on the pretext of easing ecological problems. We should be good stewards of the environment, but we should not place that responsibility in the hands of those in the United Nations who want to use it as a tool for global dominance.

Globalism Opposes the Traditional Family

What are the goals of the globalists? Although they are a diverse and eclectic group of international bankers, politicians, futurists, religious leaders, and economic planners, they are unified in their desire to unite the planet under a one-world government, a single economic system, and a one-world religion. Through various governmental programs, international conferences, and religious meetings, they desire to unite the globe into one single network.

Although this goal can be achieved in a variety of ways, the primary focus of globalists is on the next generation of young people. By pushing global education in the schools, they believe that they can indoctrinate students to accept the basic foundations of globalism. According to one globalist, global education seeks to "prepare students for citizenship in the global age." Globalists believe that this new form of education will enable future generations to deal effectively with population growth, environmental problems, international tensions, and terrorism.

Several obstacles stand in the way of the globalists' goals. Consequently, they have targeted three major institutions for elimination because their continued existence impedes globalists' designs to unite the world under a single economic, political, and social network. The three institutions under attack by globalists today are the traditional family, the Christian church, and the national government. Each institution espouses doctrines antithetical to the globalist vision; therefore, globalists argue, these institutions must be substantially modified or replaced.

The traditional family poses a threat to globalism for two reasons. First, it is still the primary socializing unit in our society. Parents pass on social, cultural, and spiritual values to their children. Many of these values—such as faith, hard work, and independence—collide with the designs of globalists, who envision a world in which tolerance for religion, dependence on a one-world global community, and international cooperation are the norm. Traditional American families do not teach these values; therefore, globalists seek to change the family.

Second, parental authority in a traditional family clearly supersedes international authority. Children in such families are taught to obey their parents. Parents, not a national or international governmental entity, have authority over their children. Globalists, therefore, see the traditional American family as an enemy, not as a friend.

Well-known humanist and globalist Ashley Montagu, speaking to a group of educators, declared, "The American family structure produces mentally ill children."[6] From his perspective, the traditional family that teaches such things as loyalty to God and country is not producing children mentally fit for the global world of the twenty-first century.

One of the reasons globalist educators advocate that childhood education begin at increasingly earlier ages is so that young children can be indoctrinated into globalism.

The earlier they can communicate their themes to children, the more likely will be the globalists' success in breaking the influence of the family.

The traditional family is just one of the institutions that globalists seek to change. We now turn our attention to globalistic attacks on the church and the nation.

Globalism Opposes Christianity and Nationalism

We have seen that globalists oppose the traditional family, but we must also be aware that the Christian church and a sense of national identity are contrary to their vision.

Globalists believe that the Christian church threatens their global program because of its belief in the authority of the Bible. Most other religious systems (as well as liberal Christianity) pose little threat. But Christians who believe in God, sin, and salvation through faith in Jesus Christ alone stand in the way of the globalist vision for a one-world religion.

The coming world religion will merge all religions and faiths into one big spiritual amalgam. Hinduism and Buddhism are syncretistic religions and can easily be merged into this one-world religion, but orthodox Christianity cannot.

Jesus taught, "I am the way, and the truth, and the life; no one comes to the Father, but through me" (John 14:6 NASB). Globalists, therefore, see Christianity as narrow, exclusive, and intolerant. Paul Brandwein even went so far as to say, "Any child who believes in God is mentally ill."[7] Belief in a personal God to which people owe allegiance and obedience cannot remain if globalists are to achieve their ultimate vision.

National governments also threaten globalism. If the

goal is to unite all peoples under one international banner, any nationalism or patriotism blocks the progress of that vision. Globalist and architect Buckminster Fuller once said, "Nationalism is the blood clot in the world's circulatory system."[8]

Among nations, the United States stands as one of the greatest obstacles to globalism. The European community has already acquiesced to regional and international plans, and other emerging nations are willingly joining the international community. By contrast, the United States remains independent in its national fervor and general unwillingness to cooperate with international standards. Until recently, Americans rejected nearly everything international, be it an international system of measurements (i.e., the metric system) or an international agency (such as the United Nations or the World Court).

The globalist solution is to promote global ideas in the schools. Dr. Pierce of Harvard University, speaking to educators in Denver, Colorado, said, "Every child in America who enters school at the age of five is mentally ill, because he comes to school with allegiance toward our elected officials, toward our founding fathers, toward our institutions, toward the preservation of this form of government."[9] The solution, therefore, is to purge these nationalistic beliefs from school children so they will come to embrace the goals of globalism.

Programs on global education, global history, and global citizenship are springing up all over the country. Children are being indoctrinated into a global way of thinking. Frequently, these programs masquerade as drug awareness programs, civics programs, or environmental programs. But their goal is the same—to break down a child's allegiance to family, church, and country and to replace this allegiance with the globalists' vision for a one-world government, a one-world economic system, and a one-world religion. The family, the church, and the national government, then, are three institutions that the globalists believe must be modified or destroyed if they are to achieve their globalist vision. Christians must, therefore, be diligent to defend these institutions.

8

Welfare Reform
Kerby Anderson

Many members of Congress have been pushing to reform the welfare system and break the cycles of illegitimacy and dependency. Changing the existing welfare system, however, will not be easy. In its more than fifty years of existence, the system has developed into a mass of bureaucratic idiosyncrasies, and experts say that the numerous institutionalized workers are likely to resist attempts at reforming either them or their routines.

Most taxpayers are skeptical that real change will take place, and they have every right to be skeptical. Since 1960, Congress has passed at least six major welfare revisions for welfare recipients to find work. But the rolls increased by 460 percent in the same period.[1] Nevertheless, welfare must be reformed. Since 1965, American taxpayers have been forced to pay 5 trillion dollars into a welfare system created to end poverty. The result? No measurable reduction in poverty. After three decades of Great Society programs to fight the war on poverty, poverty is worse.

The most visible and most cost-inefficient segment of the U.S. welfare system today is Aid for Dependent Children (AFDC). The system began in 1935 as a little-noticed part of the Social Security Act.[2] Its principal purpose was to aid widows and their children until the Social Security survivors' fund could pay out claims. More than fourteen million individuals are now on AFDC, and one in seven children is on welfare.

AFDC is not the only program of concern. In the early 1960s, the Kennedy administration proposed several other welfare programs. Their stated purposes were the admirable goals of eliminating dependency, delinquency, illegitimacy, and disability. The modern welfare state was born during the flood of Lyndon Johnson's Great Society programs aimed at the war on poverty.

But the road to utopia ran into some devastating potholes. Most social statistics indicate that the war on poverty had many casualties. The unintended consequence of these welfare programs is a system that breaks down families, traps the poor in idle frustration, and perpetuates a cycle of government dependency. Approximately half of today's AFDC recipients are mothers who have never been married to the father (or fathers) of their children. Another 40 percent are mothers whose husbands have left home. Half of the poor live in female-headed households. Welfare has not improved their lot. The poverty level has remained relatively unchanged since this system was initiated, while illegitimate births have increased more than 400 percent. In the 1960s, we declared war on poverty, and poverty won.

Good Intentions Gone Awry

The dramatic increases in the number of welfare recipients and the length of their dependency on welfare have alarmed both liberals and conservatives. But liberals and conservatives differ in their prescriptions. Liberals argue for more effective programs and for additional job training. Conservatives argue that the intractable pathologies of the welfare system (the destruction of the family unit and the fostering of dependency) are the results of large-scale governmental intervention. The conservative argument has been strengthened by the earlier research of Charles Murray in his book *Losing Ground.*[3]

Murray's thesis is that our government not only failed to win its war on poverty but also ended up taking more captives. Under the guise of making life better, it ended up making life worse for the poor. Murray said, "We tried to provide more for the poor and produced more poor instead. We tried to remove the barriers to escape from poverty and inadvertently built a trap." Murray calls for radical changes in the current welfare system, and a number of conservative proposals before Congress include various aspects of his recommendations.

Long before Murray's book provided a thorough statistical evaluation, social theorists and even casual observers could see that our current welfare system promotes dependency and destroys the family unit in three different ways.

First, welfare payments provide economic incentives for the creation of single-parent families because they provide a continuous source of income to young mothers. The welfare system was designed to assist when there was no father. But the system effectively eliminated the father entirely by tying payments to his absence.

An irresponsible man can father a child without worrying about how to provide for the child. A dedicated father with a low-paying job might feel forced to leave home so his children can qualify for more benefits. The welfare system eliminates the need for families to take any economic initiative by rewarding single parents and penalizing married couples. The result has been an illegitimate birthrate for African-American women of 88 percent.

Second, society's "adultification" of children in general contributes to welfare's poverty cycle. Various judicial rulings have undercut the role parents can have in helping their children with difficult decisions. Courts have ruled that parental notification for dispensing birth control drugs and devices violates the minors' rights. Courts have ruled that children need not obtain their parents' permission before they obtain an abortion. The natural progression of this continued trend toward children's rights is the breakdown of the family.

The most rapid rise in poverty rates have been among the children whom the system was ostensibly designed to help. The astonishing increase (over 400 percent) in illegitimate births is a principal reason for poverty and the perpetuation of a poverty cycle of "children raising children."

Third, the current welfare system rewards dependency and punishes initiative. Welfare does not require recipients to do anything in exchange for their benefits. Many rules actually discourage work and provide benefits that reduce the incentive to find work. In Maryland, for example, a single parent with two children would need to earn a minimum of $7.50 an hour to earn the same amount as provided by welfare grants and benefits.[4] Therefore, is it any wonder that so many welfare mothers conclude that staying on welfare is better than getting off?

Can Welfare Be Changed?

Although there has been much talk of welfare reform, very few substantive changes have been made in the welfare system in the last three decades. Since 1960, Congress has passed at least six major welfare revisions for welfare recipients to find work, but the rolls increased by 460 percent in the same period.

A Department of Health and Human Services report revealed that the cost of administering welfare programs grows twice as fast as the number of recipients. According to the Congressional Budget Office, welfare as a percentage of the Gross Domestic Product has increased by 230 percent, and its cost will exceed five hundred billion dollars by the end of this decade.[5]

Various congressional proposals attempt either substantially to modify or to eliminate the current system. First, let's focus on the proposals that want to modify welfare in the following five areas.

The first change would be in *child support.* Fathers are not providing child support, and this change would tighten the loopholes and make these dads pay up. Currently, unwed fathers are not named on birth certificates. The omission frequently foils attempts to collect child support. But if dad pays, then mom's welfare check does not have to be so large. The proposed bills would require the mother to identify the father in order to receive a welfare check. States could threaten deadbeat dads with garnishing wages and suspending professional licenses and driver's licenses.

The second change would be in the *marriage penalty.* If a pregnant teen gets married or lives with the father of her child, she is frequently ineligible for welfare. Congressional proposals would encourage states to abolish this "marriage penalty" and make it easier for married couples to get welfare.

Creating a *family cap* would be another significant change. Welfare mothers can increase the size of their welfare check by having more children. Congressional bills being considered would allow states to cap payments. Even if a welfare mother has another child, her check would remain the same.

In New Jersey, Arkansas, and Georgia, families already receive no increase for children born while on the dole. Congressional proposals would extend and encourage this restriction to other states. So far, the evidence is that this family cap might have some deterrence.

Another change is to emphasize *work*. Often, if a welfare mother gets a job, her check is reduced, and she is likely to lose such benefits as Medicare and free child care. The new proposals before Congress would drop benefits after two years. If an able-bodied welfare recipient does not find a private-sector job, she would be assigned a government job at minimum wage.

A final change would be to *keep teenage mothers in school*. In the current system, a teenager can receive a welfare check, get her own apartment, and drop out of school. Congressional proposals would require a teen mother to live at home until age eighteen. She would have to stay in school or lose her benefits. If the family's income is high enough, she would not receive a check at all.

These are a few of the elements of the congressional proposals to modify welfare as we know it. They take some solid steps toward ending illegitimacy and dependency. Some even more radical proposals are being discussed, and we will consider them next.

Other Congressional Proposals

Welfare is supposed to be a second chance, not a way of life. Try telling that to some children who represent the fourth generation on welfare. Proponents of radical reform believe that we must scrap the current system. There are congressional bills being considered that attempt to do more than modify the system and actually propose elimination of certain aspects of welfare.

One bill by Congressman James Talent would no longer provide welfare checks, food stamps, and public housing to women under twenty-one who have children born out of wedlock. The justification for such actions stems from the original work by Charles Murray, who believes that only this radical solution will cause teenagers to change their behavior.

Illegitimacy is the underlying cause of poverty, crime, and social meltdown in the inner cities. Proponents of these radical proposals believe that it is better to stem the tide of illegitimacy than to try building a dam of social programs to contain the later flood of problems.

Nearly a third of American children are born out of wedlock, and those children are four times more likely to be poor. The connection between illegitimacy and crime is also disturbing. More than half of the juvenile offenders serving prison time were raised by only one parent. If birthrates continue, the number of young people trapped in poverty and tempted by the values of the street will increase. Illegitimacy is essentially a ticking crime bomb.

Another reform proposal concerns the entangled bureaucracy of welfare. Currently, governors must ask the federal government if they can revamp their state welfare systems. The federal bureaucracy costs money. If you took the money spent for welfare and gave it to poor families, it would amount to twenty-five thousand dollars a year for every family of four.

Advocates of complete reform propose freezing or changing welfare payments. They would replace food stamps and AFDC with block grants to the states. Each state would then be free to design its own system.

These proposals emphasize work by providing a transition into the workplace for able-bodied welfare recipients.

The federal government would double welfare payments during the transition period but would send the check to the employer rather than directly to the welfare recipient. This change would, no doubt, provide greater incentive for recipients to work hard and stay on the job.

Many members of Congress are skeptical of proposals to provide jobs through job training programs. In the past, job training has been relatively ineffective. One 1990 study of New York welfare recipients found that 63 percent of black recipients and 54 percent of white recipients received training while on welfare, but few of them left the welfare rolls for employment. Even with the training, less than 8 percent of blacks and 5 percent of whites were working.

Finally, these proposals would also encourage marriage. Currently, the welfare system encourages fathers to leave their families. These proposals would provide not only social incentives but also economic incentives by providing two-parent families with a one-thousand-dollar tax credit.

Biblical Principles

Considering steps either to modify or to end our current welfare system should cause Christians to ask two important questions.

First, who should help the poor? The Bible clearly states that the primary agent of compassionate distribution of food and resources should be the church. Unfortunately, the majority of poverty programs in existence today are government programs or governmentally sponsored programs. Although we can applaud the excellent programs established by a few churches and Christian organizations, we must lament the fact that most poverty programs are instituted by the state.

Poverty is much more than an economic problem. It

results from psychological, social, and spiritual problems. Government agencies, by their very nature, cannot meet these needs. The church must take a much greater role in helping the poor and not be content to allow the government to be the primary agency for welfare.

Second, who should we help? Government programs help nearly everyone who falls below the poverty line, but the Bible establishes more specific qualifications. A biblical system of welfare must apply some sort of means test for potential recipients of welfare. Following are three biblical qualifications for those who should receive welfare.

1. *They must be poor.* They should be unable to meet basic human needs without outside assitance. We should help those who have suffered misfortune or persecution, but the Bible does not instruct us to give to anyone who asks for help or to those who are merely trying to improve their comfort or lifestyle.

2. *They must be diligent.* Some people are poor because of laziness, neglect, or gluttony. Christians are instructed to admonish laziness and poor habits, such as alcohol or drug abuse, that lead to poverty. Proverbs 6:6 says, "Go to the ant, you sluggard, observe her ways and be wise" (NASB). More pointedly, the apostle Paul says, "If anyone will not work, neither let him eat" (2 Thess. 3:10 NASB). Lazy people should not be rewarded by welfare but rather encouraged to change their ways.

3. The church must provide for those thrown into poverty because of the *death of the family provider.* The Bible commands us to provide for widows and orphans who are in need (James 1:27). Paul wrote to Timothy that a widow who was sixty years or older and whose only husband had died was qualified to be supported by the church (1 Tim. 5:9).

The church can and should meet the needs of the poor.[6] Churches and individual Christians must do their part in fighting poverty in their area. Homemakers can provide meals. Educators can provide tutoring and counseling. Businesspeople can provide employment training. The church as a whole can provide everything from a full-time ministry to the poor to an occasional collection for the benevolence fund to be distributed to those facing temporary needs brought about by illness or unemployment. The key is for the church to obey God's command to feed the hungry and clothe the naked. Helping the poor is not an option. We have a biblical responsibility that we cannot simply pass off to the government.

Part 2
Education Issues

Worldviews and Education

Don Closson

A nswers to the important questions about education, such as curricular content, teaching methodology, and student-teacher relationships, depend upon one's worldview. A worldview is comprised of the truths that a person holds by faith concerning the fundamental questions facing everyone everywhere. All people hold faith positions or beliefs about the nature of reality, human nature, the nature of right and wrong, the nature of knowledge, what happens at death, and the direction of history. An individual's worldview defines his or her notion of what the "good life" is and, in turn, influences how he or she views the ideal educational setting.

In the last decade, America has experienced a heated debate about the role, function, and organization of its schools. Dr. Allan Bloom, a University of Chicago professor, wrote *The Closing of the American Mind* about the state of higher education in America in the late 1980s. Although it was a rather academic work written mainly for his colleagues, it provoked a national firestorm of debate. Measured by the number of articles and books written in response to it (and the fact that it was a best-seller for months), it was one of those rare books that defined a national discussion. Bloom's main contention was that students no longer believe in truth or the ability of books or schools to supply them with truth. They have become flat souled, left only with a self-centered nicety that gives them no reason *not* to conform to the ideas and behaviors that popular culture imposes on them.

Dr. Ronald H. Nash, a professor at Reformed Seminary, responded to Bloom's ideas in his book *The Closing of the American Heart.* Although Nash agrees with much of Dr. Bloom's critique, he offers a different set of solutions to the problems facing education in America.

Both Bloom and Nash agree that ideas have consequences. Bloom believes, contrary to popular notions of relativism, that a serious life of the mind includes coming to an understanding of the alternative worldviews that are available. He also believes that choosing between the various worldviews holds "great risk with consequences that are hard to bear."[1] Nash goes one step further. He proposes that Christians need to instruct their children within the framework of a Christian worldview, the foundation upon which all of the disciplines should rest. In other words, both of these men argue that education cannot be neutral; it must stand for something. Someone must decide what it means to be an educated person and, consequently, what students should know and believe when they graduate from our schools. Education can never be neutral because no individual has a neutral worldview. Public policy is shaped by the ultimate concerns of those holding power in our society. Worldviews shape institutions and policies and directly affect how our children are educated.

What frightens Bloom and Nash is that although the public schools are often promoted as a marketplace of ideas, relativism (especially concerning ethical issues) has become a functional monopoly. Schools of education, teachers' unions, administrators' organizations, and textbooks have methodically divested themselves of viewpoints that hold to supernatural explanations or that uphold the necessity of moral absolutes. By embracing naturalism, educational leaders see themselves as neutral players in the cultural war raging in our society.

As R. C. Sproul explains in the foreword to Nash's book, modern education has abandoned truth and replaced it with rhetoric. Educators have become modern-day Sophists. Speaking the truth is less important than convincing others that something is true, regardless of whether it actually is. As in ancient Greece, "preference replaces laws, personal gratification replaces virtue, and truth is slain in the streets."[2]

Moral Relativism

Bloom opens his book thus: "There is one thing a professor can be absolutely certain of: almost every student entering the university believes, or says he believes, that truth is relative."[3] This now-famous (or infamous) description of American students rests on his observation that a single way of thinking has come to dominate our campuses. Relativism, the view that truth and absolute values (other than tolerance and openness) do not exist, is the governing mechanism by which people solve moral dilemmas in our institutions of higher learning. Bloom adds that this assurance that truth does not exist has left our students with little desire to seek knowledge. The search for truth has been replaced by what Bloom calls an "insubstantial awareness that there are many cultures."[4] Because cultures have different values, truth must not exist. From this they derive the maxims that we should just get along with one another and that no values are superior to any others or worth defending. Students are left with a gentle egotism, a desire for comfort.

Bloom believes that the shallowness of our students' position has been caused by the reluctance of those in charge of their education to furnish their minds with something more substantial than MTV and the most recent slasher movie. Without the aid of substantial books and without heroes that literature can provide, students lack the resources to fight conformity in a world that denies any basis for virtue.

Three Forms of Illiteracy

Dr. Nash generally agrees with the dismal picture that Bloom drew, claiming that schools have left our students with three kinds of illiteracy: functional, cultural, and moral. *Functional illiteracy* is the inability to understand the written word well enough to function within our society. Nash gives evidence of a major problem. About 13 percent of all seventeen-year-olds are functionally illiterate, as are 24 million adults, a remarkable number considering that most people have a high school diploma today. In 1910, only 2.2 percent of American children between the ages of ten and fourteen could neither read nor write.[5] Nash quotes Karl Shapiro at the University of California, Davis:

> What is really distressing is that this generation cannot and does not read. I am speaking of university students in what are supposed to be our best universities. Their illiteracy is staggering. . . . We are experiencing a literacy breakdown, which is unlike anything I know of in the history of letters.[6]

Cultural illiteracy describes the student who can read but is unable to thrive in the modern world because he or she lacks the background information necessary to interpret the material read. The most outspoken and recognized advocate for cultural literacy is Dr. E. D. Hirsch Jr., author of a best-selling book on the topic. Both he and Nash charge that modern educational theory deserves much of the blame for causing cultural illiteracy. Hirsch contends that educators have accepted a false belief that children will develop the necessary intellectual and social skills to function in our society without regard to the specific content of an educational program. Educators are more interested in *how* children learn rather than in *what* they learn. Therefore, children often fail to store away enough information to become culturally literate.

Educators will grudgingly admit the problem of functional and cultural literacy, and occasionally they will assume some of the blame, but Nash believes that they are actually proud of the decline in moral literacy. Nash sees the problem of *moral illiteracy* as a cultural war between those who are religious and support traditional virtues and those who are secular and advocate modernist or postmodernist values. Those in the midst of the battle understand this conflict whereas the typical American does not.

The problem of moral illiteracy is becoming a widely recognized problem. Jewish scholar Will Herberg writes,

> We are surrounded on all sides by the wreckage of our great intellectual tradition. In this kind of spiritual chaos, neither freedom nor order is possible. Instead of freedom, we have the all-engulfing whirl of pleasure and power; instead of order, we have the

jungle wilderness of normlessness and self-indulgence.[7]

At the turn of the century, John Dewey, the most revered of American philosophers, sought to break education away from anything premodern, any authority—be it the church, the Bible, or supernatural reality—of any kind. It became the responsibility of educators to eliminate values that were derived from any source that was not scientific. The result has been devastating. John Silber, president of Boston University states,

> In recent years, in contrast, our society has become increasingly secular and the curriculum of the public schools has been denuded of almost all ethical content. As a result universities must confront a student body ignorant of the evidence and arguments that underlie and support many of our traditional moral principles and practices.[8]

Self-Actualized Children

In an attempt to break with premodern traditions and virtues, educators turned to nondirective, affective education in the 1960s and 1970s. Values clarification techniques (Sidney Simon) and moral reasoning skills (Lawrence Kolhberg) were used to break the transmission of values from parents to their children. Psychologist Carl Rogers and others taught that to become self-actualized adults, children must reject the absolute religious values they have been taught at home or church. Students must seek values within themselves. Educators are to be facilitators, helping students to discover their own values, not transmitters of the virtues that Western civilization has cherished through the centuries. Students were convinced slowly that moral issues are rarely solved by a "right" answer. The constant use of moral dilemmas, presenting students with extremely difficult moral problems that even adults are unable to solve, eventually broke down students' confidence in the moral truths taught in the home or church.

The movement that began as encounter groups, Gestalt therapy, and other self-help techniques in the 1960s had become part of the public school curriculum. This model of teacher as therapist proceeded to replace the idea of teacher as scholar and has been defended as the only solution to the very real problems of teen pregnancy, drug use, suicide, and other issues. But even one of its early adherents, Dr. W. M. Coulson, a colleague of Carl Rogers and Abraham Maslow, voiced the dangers of using these techniques on school children and of having unqualified teachers become therapists.[9]

The changes that occurred in the 1960s and 1970s in both society and higher education left our schools with an aversion to and a fear of moral truth. The idea that human beings bear the image of their Creator is foreign to those who write textbooks and often to those who teach our children. When educators do talk about the need for values in our schools, they are usually referring to cultural constructs, man-made rules that have meaning only to the cultural group that gives them authority. As our country experiences greater cultural diversity, we are left without a consensus about what to teach and with which virtues to train our children. In this environment, students naturally perceive that they have no responsibility to learn the heritage of our culture or to abide by the virtues that built it.

A Worldview Shift

We began this chapter by noting how influential one's worldview is in determining the process and content of education. This century has seen a dramatic shift in the worldview assumptions from which public school educators operate. The biggest shift has been the replacing of a God-centered reality with what is often called philosophical naturalism. Naturalism is the assertion that God or anything supernatural does not exist. This was the philosophical beginning point for John Dewey and Edward Thorndike, who, along with many others, were the founders of the progressive education movement in the first half of this century. From that initial point of philosophical naturalism, a number of other foundational beliefs have followed. First is the view that human beings are autonomous creatures possessing neither moral truth nor moral responsibility to anything or anyone other than themselves. Second, naturalists argue that the only source of knowledge or truth is via the scientific method. All other sources of knowledge, such as religious truth or artistic beauty, are mere opinions.

This quasi-religious devotion to the scientific method argues that any belief that cannot be tested by science is at best meaningless. But, as J. P. Moreland has pointed out, faith in science itself must be defended at the worldview level. Moreland writes, "The aims, methodologies, and presuppositions of science cannot be validated by science. One cannot turn to science to justify science any more than one can pull oneself up by his own bootstraps."[10] In other words, the scientific method cannot be used to justify faith in the scientific method.

This inclination toward naturalism has caused some educators to consider their students maladjusted or even mentally ill if they hold to a competing worldview such as Christian theism. As the courts have systematically filtered out Christian thought and imposed a high wall of separation between church and state, students are often left with the impression that naturalism is the only academically acceptable worldview.

Bloom's Solution

As we have noted, Bloom sees relativism as a powerful enemy of our students' minds and a force that is undermining our educational system. His antidote lies in one major recommendation. Bloom explains,

> The only serious solution is the one that is almost universally rejected: the good old Great Books approach, in which a liberal education means reading certain generally recognized classic texts, just reading them, letting them dictate what the questions are and the method of approaching them—not forcing them into categories we make up, not treating them as historical products, but trying to read them as their authors wished them to be read.[11]

Bloom wants university students to let the minds of the past, particularly the philosophers, speak directly to today's students without having to go through the modern critiques of feminism, Marxism, and other ideologies. At best, anything written before the modern scientific age is suspect.

Nash agrees that the great books are valuable and contribute to a complete education, but he believes that the array of ideas contained in them will baffle students unless they have an overarching philosophy to guide them through the maze. Although Bloom acknowledges the necessity for individuals and schools to make the hard choices about the big questions in life, he himself fails to do so in regard to a curriculum. Should teachers treat all of the great books equally? Because the authors of the great books disagree intensely on basic issues regarding the nature of reality and humanity, are we not promoting a new relativism in place of the old? Do we accept Augustine's *Confessions* and his views on the sinfulness of mankind or Rousseau's *Confessions,* which posits a naturally good human nature?

Nash contends that one condition of being an educated person is having a single, unified world and life view, something not found in the great books. As Christian philosopher Gordon Clark once put it, "If someone wishes to unify education, it is not enough to say that a philosophical base is necessary. To accomplish such a result, it is essential to provide the philosophy."[12] Only Christian theism can accomplish adequately the task of unification.

Human beings are never neutral concerning the nature of God, and what people believe to be true will ultimately affect their view of education. Although Bloom talks about how modern education has impoverished the souls of today's students, he leaves us without any indication of how those souls should be fed or what connection should be made between knowledge and virtue.

Socrates and Plato warned against the inadequacies of an education that taught people only how to select the best means to achieve their ends or goals. It was far more important, they thought, that humans recognize the importance of selecting the right ends. But the subject of right, good, or noble ends is precisely what contemporary education seeks to avoid. In Nash's words,

> While the Bible does not teach physics or astronomy, it does provide a structure for human thought, a perspective on reality. The biblical perspective can, among other things, inform us of the limitations and proper aims of theoretical inquiry. It tells us that the pursuit of knowledge, while important, is not the sum total of human life.[13]

Nash makes some general recommendations to parents who are concerned about their children's education. The first such recommendation is to revitalize the educational role of the family. As J. Gresham Machen once wrote, "The most important Christian education institution is not the pulpit or the school . . . it is the Christian family. And that institution has to a very large extent ceased to do its work."[14] Even Allan Bloom, by no means an evangelical Christian, blamed the current condition of education on the demise of family influence on our children's education.

Parents must be actively involved in seeing that their children mature theologically and intellectually. Theologically, children need to know what they believe. Our children need to learn to love God with their minds, as Matthew 22:37 calls all Christians to do. To love God with our minds, we must know something about Him. Families need to work together to develop Christian minds in their children, minds that can apply Christian truth to every area of life. Intellectually, we must avoid the common practice of compartmentalizing knowledge into sacred and secular components. This division is unbiblical and leads to the dangerous notion that secular knowledge is somehow unfit for the spiritual Christian.

Nash also calls for greater local control of schools as a way for Christians to fight the hostile attitudes that prevail against biblical thought on campus. Parental choice and vouchers take this concept one step further. The bottom line is that parents cannot assume that the education they received in the 1950s or 1960s is still being delivered in our schools today. The current educational techniques and dogmas that have come to dominate education have serious problems. Parents must get involved by applying discernment to the decisions of how and where their children will be educated.

10

Education and Choice

Don Closson

Most parents are aware that a good education is fundamental to financial, professional, and personal success. Some parents might have greater resources or a more precise picture of how to accomplish this goal than others, but studies indicate that Americans from all socio-economic, ethnic, and racial groups want their children to be well educated. If this is true, why are so many of our students doing so poorly?

Recent research has discovered that after the socio-economic well-being and educational level of the parents, the next most important variable predicting student success is the way in which a school is organized. Effective schools have strong educational leaders who possess a clear vision of what it means to be an educated person and who have the power to assemble a staff of like-minded teachers. These schools set high academic standards and encourage the belief that, with few exceptions, children are capable of achieving at these levels. They encourage collegial and professional staff relationships and establish a disciplined learning environment.[1]

An example of an effective school, functioning in some of the most difficult of circumstances, is the Westside Preparatory School in Chicago, Illinois. Marva Collins, its founder, has proven that when the preceding characteristics exist in a school, students from inner-city, low-income, single-parent families can achieve as well as those from the suburbs. In describing her inner-city program, she states, "The expectations are as high here as in the most nurtured suburban area." Her motto for the children is, "We are known by our deeds, not our needs."[2]

If we know what makes a school effective, how do we go about converting the vast number of ineffective schools, many of which are in our nation's cities, into high-performance schools? The expensive reforms of the last few decades have yielded marginal results. Between 1960 and 1990, a great deal of money and effort went into school reforms. Total expenditures went from 67.5 billion to 205.3 billion in constant dollars.[3] Much of the money was allocated for the two areas most often noted as fundamental to better schools: increased teachers' salaries, which have increased 25 percent in constant dollars since 1960, and reduced class size.[4] By most indicators, including scholastic aptitude test (SAT) scores, however, these efforts have failed to produce more effective schools.

In a very influential study funded by the Brookings Institution, John Chubb and Terry Moe found that the greatest hindrance to effective schooling is bureaucracy.[5] Conversely, the most important ingredient for establishing effective schools is autonomy. Few public schools have autonomy; many private schools do. They argue that the key to educational reform is finding a mechanism that will allow for school autonomy while maintaining a sufficient amount of public accountability.

The One Best System?

The current democratic system of governing our schools exposes them to special interest groups at the local, state, and federal levels. Acquired immune deficiency sydrome (AIDS) awareness educators, bilingual teachers, vocational programs, and various ethnic groups have their lobbyists, each advocating program expansion and higher spending and often using the courts to impose their will. Local school boards, state legislators, and the federal government respond to pressure from their constituents by enacting regulations that local schools must observe. Instead of being an educational leader, the local principal often becomes a middle manager much more concerned about following regulations than enacting a personal vision of educational excellence.

John Chubb and Terry Moe recommend educational vouchers as the most effective tool for reducing bureaucratic regulations and for freeing schools and school leaders to pursue academic excellence. A voucher plan promises to produce more autonomous schools because it inverts the way schools are controlled. Decision-making authority would be decentralized, returning local principals to the role of educational leaders. The influence of outside interest groups such as unions and state legislatures would be diminished. Schools would be held accountable by the market system; if they fail to attract students, they will go out of business.

The concept of a voucher plan is relatively simple. The government would determine how much money it is willing to spend per student in the state or district. Parents would then receive a voucher for that amount for each of their children. Parents would then select a school for each of their children, and the school (or schools) would redeem the vouchers for state funds.

A key attribute of vouchers is that they give parents in our worst school districts a choice of where to send their children. If local public schools are dangerous or fail to educate, a choice or voucher plan would give parents the freedom to move their children to a better environment. In 1989, Milwaukee, Wisconsin, became the first example of an urban center to adopt the choice mechanism for school reform. Today, thousands of economically disadvantaged students are receiving vouchers to attend private schools. Recently, the program was expanded to allow participation by private religious schools.

Throughout the last decade, a pitched battle has been going on between voucher advocates and the teachers' unions. Although attempts to enact statewide voucher plans in Colorado and California failed by large margins, Florida recently managed to pass the first statewide choice program, which will provide $4,000 scholarships for children in failing schools to attend public or private schools.[6] Other states are focusing on ways that vouchers might help the most needy students at the worst schools. The goal of reformers is not to replace public schools but to make them better. It is argued that competition will cause schools to become more responsive to the parents they are serving rather than to other outside interest groups.

Schools become more effective when they are autonomous from bureaucratic regulations. Reformers on both sides of the political fence have suggested educational choice via vouchers as the best way to produce autonomous schools and, thus, more effective schools.

Objections to School Choice

Although some progress has been made in the last ten years, very few families have the opportunity to participate in a voucher or choice program. The greatest opposition to vouchers has come from the teachers' unions (the National

Education Association [NEA] and the American Federation of Teachers [AFT]), the Parent-Teacher Association (PTA), and other groups that might lose money, power, or prestige if parents are given greater choice in how their children are educated. The NEA worked hard and spent large sums of money to defeat choice legislation in Colorado and California. Let's consider some of the specific objections that opponents use against vouchers.

A recent bill, which President William Clinton vetoed, was a federally funded voucher plan that would have given two thousand scholarships of up to $3,200 each to children from low-income families in the District of Columbia. What were some typical antivoucher arguments, and how might we respond to them?

One objection is that vouchers will undermine the unity of America that has been created and maintained by tax-supported common schools. The original ideal espoused by Horace Mann was that students of all socioeconomic classes would be schooled together and that this would create mutual respect. Unfortunately, public schools are extremely segregated by both race and economics. The wealthy are able to purchase homes in elite suburban school districts whereas others are trapped in schools that are unsuccessful and often filled with violence and crime. Washington, D.C., schools, for example, are highly segregated by race and class. Only 4 percent of the students are white, and 94 percent of them qualify for free or reduced-priced lunches because of their low family income.[7] Choice would actually help to recreate the common school notion. Parents could decide where to place their children in school regardless of geography and, as a result, the schools would become more accountable to local control.

Another criticism against choice might be called the

"incompetent parent argument." Some critics think that parents of minority or lower-income students will not know the difference between good schools and poor schools; thus, they will get stuck in second-rate schools. They argue that the best students will be siphoned off and that the difficult students will remain, creating a two-tiered education system. Other critics are afraid that poor parents are not used to making important decisions or will make schooling choices based on athletics rather than academics.

In response, one must note that many of the schools that these children attend are already the worst in the nation; choice can only better their educational environment, even if the choice is made for the wrong reason. Jonathan Kozal's book *Savage Inequalities* has documented just how bad many of these schools are.[8] For example, the District of Columbia's average scores on the National Assessment of Education Progress tests are the lowest in the nation,[9] this in spite of the fact that per pupil spending there is $8,290 compared with a national average of $5,528. Money alone is not the answer! Choice would allow parents to opt for schools that are using their resources productively.

Another objection to choice is the "selectivity argument." Critics contend that choice will help only those children who are moved to better schools by their parents. They demand that if any children are to be helped by a reform, all children must be helped. A U.S. Secretary of Education has stated, "If a school is failing, the solution isn't to give 50 scholarships to 50 children and leave 500 behind, but to fix the whole school."[10] This "selectivity argument" is one of the most frequently used criticisms against private schools and choice.

Arguing that we should not help some students succeed until we can help all students succeed seems remarkably hardhearted. Could it be that these critics are giving
up the "good" for the "perfect"? Although it is true that
many private schools have high standards for admissions,
many of them have been serving disadvantaged urban children for years. The Varnett School in Houston, Texas, has
built a reputation for working with students whom the
public schools have failed, and the work of Marva Collins
in Chicago shows that private schools can succeed with all
types of students from low-income urban settings. Soci-
ologist James Coleman has documented how Catholic
schools have succeeded in raising the academic achievement
of students who do poorly in public schools, including
African-Americans, Hispanics, and a variety of children
from low socio-economic backgrounds. Because the proposed legislation in Washington would provide vouchers
for only low-income students, it cannot be charged with
pulling out only the wealthy.

Another concern that many people have regarding
vouchers might be called the "radical schools scare." Some
opponents contend that vouchers will open the doors to
"cult schools" or schools run by right-wing bigots. Others
fear that vouchers might encourage societal tribalism and
schools that teach nontraditional subject matter.

Will there be a market for schools that are somehow
bizarre or extremist? Private colleges in America are schools
of choice, receive government funds, and are considered
world class. Having to compete for existence quickly weeds
out schools that fail to educate. Of course, any choice plan
would allow the government to protect parents against
educational fraud and from schools that fail to do what
they advertise they will do, although one wonders why

this standard doesn't apply to many of our public schools today that are failing to educate so many of their students.

In many minds, the idea that tax money might end up in the hands of a Christian school is enough to veto any choice plan. To them, this represents a clear violation of church-state separation. In fact, the church-state argument is not a very strong one. The federal government provides Pell grants to students at private religious-affiliated colleges and the GI Bill covers tuition at seminaries. Yale law professor Stephen Carter points out,

> For the government to subsidize some private schools but refuse to subsidize the religious ones would make religious schools more costly and would thus constitute a government created disincentive to use them. In other areas of constitutional law, we do not call such disincentives "neutrality"; we call them "discrimination."[11]

Many Christians think that government intervention will follow public vouchers. But even if Christian schools refuse to participate, many other children will benefit from new, more effective schools that will be competing for their tuition vouchers—schools that Christians might begin as a ministry to those suffering in our troubled cities.

Other Mechanisms for Creating Effective Schools

The threat of vouchers has resulted in the passing of charter school legislation in a number of states. In 1993, Colorado passed the Charter Schools Act, which allows the creation of publicly funded schools operated by parents, teachers, and/or community members under a charter or contract with a local school district. A charter school is defined by the legislature as a "semiautonomous public school of choice within a school district." Lawmakers are beginning to recognize that for schools to be effective they must be autonomous. As a result, charter schools can request waivers from district and state regulations that interfere with their vision.

California and Minnesota have also passed charter legislation. Minnesota's program is a good example of why charter laws are more a political response to the voucher threat than a real attempt to free schools from excessive bureaucracy. In that state, charter schools must be started by licensed teachers, who must comprise a majority of the board. They must also meet state education standards called outcomes. Charter schools may establish their own budget and establish curricula, but the goals of individual schools will be dictated by the state. The statewide teachers' union would be a powerful force within these teacher-controlled schools.

Another plan for creating stronger schools revolves around private vouchers. In 1991, J. Patrick Rooney, Chairman of the Board of the Golden Rule Insurance Company, convinced his organization to pledge $1.2 million for the next three years to fund half the private school tuition for approximately five hundred Indianapolis, Indiana, students. To qualify, the students must be eligible for free or reduced-priced lunches according to federal guidelines. By 1993, the program had placed more than one thousand students in eighty schools.

Inspired by Rooney's concept, James R. Leininger of San Antonio, Texas, created the Children's Educational Opportunity Foundation, which has gathered $1.5 million in pledges from various Texas businesses. Off-shoot groups are starting in Austin, Albany, Denver, Phoenix, and Dallas. The Center for the Study of Education Reform at the University of North Texas has conducted an analysis on the effects of these private voucher initiatives and found that parents are extremely satisfied with the program even though they fund only half of the cost of their children's private education.

Although both charter schools and private choice programs attempt to create more effective schools by encouraging autonomy, both ideas have limitations. Charter schools' survival depend on the very bureaucracy that creates ineffective schools, and private vouchers are limited to the good will of corporations willing to invest in them. This leaves publicly funded choice through vouchers as the best hope for widespread, significant change.

Christians should not limit their interest in this debate to their own family's educational needs. God told His people who were held captive in Babylon to "seek the welfare of the city where I have sent you into exile, and pray to the LORD on its behalf; for in its welfare you will have welfare" (Jer. 29:7 NASB). Our concern should be the welfare, and thus the education, of *all* children in our nation.

11

Public, Private, or Home Education

Don Closson

Americans seem to be consumed by the idea of choice. But choice can be a burden as well as a blessing. Many Christian parents are confronted today with the complicated choice of how best to educate their children. As the moral standards in our society move farther and farther from biblical standards, the importance of choice looms ever larger.

In a recent conversation, this dilemma became even more evident to me. My friends' daughter was about to enter high school. She was bright and concerned about living as a Christian. But her parents were afraid that her desire to be part of the "in" group and to be accepted could cause her to be influenced negatively by her peers.

The public high school in town was very good, above average in many ways. It offered a good academic program and a wide variety of activities. But these parents had some important reservations about sending their daughter there. Like most other Christians, they were aware that public schools, by law, are supposed to maintain strict neutrality concerning religious topics. Many school administrators interpret this to mean that anything relating to a Christian worldview is to be removed from the classroom.

My friends were also aware that the ethical standards they hold and that are central to the upbringing of their children are considered unusual by most of the students, teachers, and other parents in the community, and that this attitude would place an added burden on their daughter.

They did not feel capable of home schooling, although they were sympathetic with the philosophy of that movement. A Christian school was available, but it was an hour's drive away and represents a substantial financial commitment, especially with college tuition looming ahead.

These friends, like many other people, were trying to sort through one of the more perplexing dilemmas facing our nation's parents. By what criteria should parents choose their children's schools?

Education is a fairly emotional topic; we all tend to return to our own mental images of what it means to be schooled. Some people remember public schooling as a joyous time with Christian teachers and a peer group that resulted in lifelong friendships. Others might remember a private school setting that was overly restrictive, resulting in a negative experience. But should we make the decision of how to educate our children today based on how things were twenty or thirty years ago, even in the same school system?

A helpful book titled *Schooling Choices: An Examination of Private, Public, and Home Education,* edited by H. Wayne House, allows three advocates to argue for their favorite schooling environment. Each man professes Christianity. David Smith, a superintendent of schools in Indiana when the book was published, argues for parents making use of our public schools. Kenneth Gangel, a professor at Dallas Theological Seminary, defends the Christian school. Greg Harris, now with Nobel Publishing and formerly the director of Christian Life Workshops, promotes home-schooling. The book offers no conclusions; instead, the issues are developed by the proponents themselves and then critiqued by the other two writers.

If we assume that Christian parents have a God-given responsibility to raise and educate their children in a manner that glorifies God, this discussion of educational choices becomes central to our parenting task. My own children have experienced all three forms of educational institutions. But rather than simplifying the dilemma, this experience, as well as my background as a public school teacher and administrator, has taught me to hesitate in telling a parent that there is one best educational environment for every child in all circumstances.

Biblical Evidence

Supporting the Christian school setting, Gangel argues that all of a child's education should be Bible-centered. Ephesians 6:4 states, "Fathers, do not exasperate your children; instead, bring them up in the training and instruction of the Lord." If we tell our children to live biblically but train them in a secular setting, we may indeed exasperate them. The question goes beyond sheltering our children from a classroom that is openly hostile to Christianity. Even a neutral approach, if that were possible, would be insufficient. The whole teaching environment must be centered on a Christian worldview.

A public school superintendent, Smith thinks that Gangel's view is not necessarily true. Quoting Luke 8:16 and Matthew 28:19–20, he prompts Christians to be salt and light and to fulfill the Great Commission in the public schools. Smith endorses a public schooling experience as a way of strengthening our children and preparing them to be witnesses for Christ in the real world.

Gangel replies that nowhere does the Bible say, "Give a child twelve years of training in the way he should not go, and he will be made strong by it."[1] Instead, God tells us, "Train a child in the way he should go, and when he is old he will not turn from it."[2]

Both Gangel and Harris emphasize the importance of peer influence or companionship. Both of them quote Proverbs 13:20—"He who walks with the wise grows wise, but a companion of fools suffers harm"—and 1 Corinthians 15:33—"Do not be deceived: 'bad company corrupts good morals'" (NASB). It seems clear that our children's closest companions are to view morality biblically.

Luke 6:40 states, "Everyone, after he has been fully trained, will be like his teacher" (NASB). Although Smith thinks that public school teachers are a conservative group and that many of them are Christians, both Gangel and Harris think that having a Christian teacher is a requirement that should not be left to chance. Greg Harris goes one step further, arguing that parents are in the best position to teach and be companions to their children.

Another major concern is the nature of knowledge and true wisdom. If we believe that "the fear of the LORD is the beginning of wisdom" (Prov. 9:10) and that "in [Christ] are hidden all the treasures of wisdom and knowledge" (Col. 2:3), then the ability of a public school to give our children a true perspective on the way things really are is placed in question. Perhaps public schools could function as vocational education centers, but even then moral questions would be involved.

Although we can see how Christian public school teachers might influence their students, they will be in constant conflict with textbooks that assume a naturalistic viewpoint and a curriculum that steers clear of controversy. Harris argues that nothing will kill the zeal of a Christian teacher quicker than a public school setting. He believes that many Christians imagine that they are having a quiet impact and rationalize that someday the fruit will be more visible when, in fact, they are promoting a non-Christian worldview by dividing their professional life from their Christian faith.

Both Harris and Gangel argue that Christians must integrate their beliefs with all of their activities. This task is becoming increasingly more difficult in the public school setting, where textbooks, self-esteem programs, drug- and sex-education curricula, and teachers' unions have adopted a view of humanity and morality that portrays human-kind as autonomous from God.

Spiritual Benefits

As Christian parents, we want more than anything else for our children to become spiritually mature. While rec-ognizing that their own free will is the greatest factor in their future growth, the Bible does give us hope that training in righteousness now will pay off later.[3]

While admitting that one environment is not neces-sarily the best for all students, Smith thinks that young people can develop a mature Christian walk in our public schools. In fact, he states that some Christian schools and homeschools might be doing more harm than good. Be-cause of their narrow, authoritarian, and defensive views toward society, some Christian parents might retard their children's spiritual and educational development. He believes that these parents are building high emotional walls between themselves and the rest of the evangelical community. Two authors whom he spotlights for having encouraged such a view are Phyllis Schlafly and Tim LaHaye.[4]

Harris, on the other hand, sees the homeschool as a vehicle for restoring the home as the center of life and faith. Our children can be nurtured in the warmth and security of the home while they are still developing spiritually and emotionally. Once their confidence has been built concerning who they are and what they believe, then they are better prepared for the cruel elements of life. Harris also argues that by not placing our children in an age-segregated setting, they will be less peer-oriented.

Gangel believes that Christian schools will teach our children that God's program of joy in Christ supersedes the world's program of pleasure. He points to Romans 12:2 and the admonition that we are not to be conformed to this world but transformed by the renewing of our minds. This transformation of our minds should take place in all areas of life, including morality and our personal concept of truth. Christian schools afford moments during which biblical discussions of these topics are encouraged, not ridiculed.

Although some people might believe that a Christian school shelters its students from the real world, Gangel thinks that just the opposite is true. Sheltering occurs when one is taught that humans are basically good and that sin is not our most pressing problem. The fact that parents want to remove their children from a setting where drugs and violence are common is not sheltering—it's common sense.

The question posed by these writers seems to be simple: Is it better to educate our children in an environment potentially hostile to the Christian faith or to train them in one that holds exclusively to that view? I do not think that any of the writers would argue that we should not see the public schools as a potential mission field. The difference is that Smith wants our children to be the missionaries whereas the other two writers think that only well-grounded adults (and occasionally a rare student) are capable of making an impact without compromising their faith.

Will a child mature more in an exclusively Christian setting or in one governed by secular standards? My personal belief is that it depends greatly on the spiritual maturity of the child. If a student understands the nature of the spiritual battle occurring in our society, and is being equipped both at home and at church with the ammunition needed to withstand the inevitable onslaught, then his or her faith will probably grow. But how many of our young children fit this description? And how many parents are willing to risk their children becoming casualties before they have had the benefit of as much Christian training as possible?

Educational Advantages

Smith believes that the key to understanding public schools and their ability to educate is tied to the task that public schools have been given. All children are admitted to public schools, regardless of ability or background. He argues that while we are graduating a higher percentage of our young people than ever before, the average student is more proficient in both reading and computing than in the past. He claims that the literacy rate today is much higher than in earlier years.[5]

In response to the accusations that other industrialized countries score higher on similar tests, Smith refers to work done by Dr. Torstein Husen, chairman of the International Association for the Evaluation of Achievement, who concludes that these tests are often not valid comparisons.[6] As for the Japanese, Smith would argue that it is the cultural differences in regard to the work ethic, not the educational systems themselves, that produce better results.[7]

Finally, Smith states that "for the overwhelming majority of children public schools offer the best techniques, curriculum and extracurricular opportunities: in short, the most comprehensive education available."[8] Although studies have shown that the large, well-established private schools do an admirable job of teaching their affluent, middle-class clientele, we know little about the effectiveness of the newer, more fundamentalist Christian schools.

Gangel and others have challenged this assumption. Spending per student in our public schools is higher than that of any of our main industrial competitors, all of whom outscore our students on international tests. Comparisons with other countries and most private schools point to an inferior product.[9] Even those who support public schools often place their children in private schools when they have the option. Although Congress has thus far blocked vouchers that would help our nation's poorest students to attend private schools, 50 percent of the members of the Senate and 34 percent of the members of the House sent their children to private schools in 1997.[10] One study points out that if cost were not a factor, 31 percent of parents who send their children to public schools would change to private schools.[11] Even public school teachers see the value of a private education. In Cleveland, 53 percent of public school teachers send their own children to private schools, as do 49 percent in Boston and 40 percent in Los Angeles.[12]

The reason for the superiority of Christian schools,

according to Gangel, is that they are more focused than public schools. They have made a commitment to the basics of reading, writing, and math. They are not trying to be all things to all people, which is often the demand placed upon public schools. Smaller classes, a consistent philosophy of education, and strict discipline more than make up for whatever is lacking in facilities and equipment.

Gangel's argument for private schools has recently been supported by a secular source. A Brookings Institution study titled *Politics, Markets, and America's Schools* argues that public schools are unable to teach effectively because of a lack of autonomy.[13] Too many political forces are demanding that schools solve our society's most unyielding social ills. As a result, the mission and focus of our public schools have been blurred.

Harris is not shy about his support of teaching our children at home. He asserts that homeschooling yields better results in less time and with less money than the alternative systems. He believes that the superiority of homeschooling is based on two principles. The first principle is the advantage of tutoring over classroom instruction. Tutors are much more able to focus on the student's work, give immediate feedback, and adjust the work to an appropriate difficulty level. Parents who focus on the individual learning styles of their children can fashion a curriculum that plays to the child's strengths, rather than forcing the child to conform to a fixed program.

The second principle is that of delight-directed studies. Parents can focus on that in which the students are actually interested and use that natural curiosity to motivate the students. Content at an early age is not as important as developing a taste for the process of study and learning.

Another very important aspect of homeschooling is character development. Harris contends that character is caught, not taught, and that the character of the teacher is of utmost importance. Whereas the courts have stated that the behavior of public school teachers outside of the school setting is not relevant to their classroom duties, homeschooling assures that a consistent model will be presented to the student.

Because of the controversy over self-esteem curricula that use relaxation techniques very similar to transcendental meditation and yoga practices, many parents are willing to take on the task of homeschooling to avoid their children being forced to take part in therapy they deem harmful. Also, increasingly more evidence is accumulating that the drug- and sex-education programs used in our schools are breaking down parental and religious barriers to dangerous activities and replacing them with the incredible peer pressure of our youth culture.

Another concern for all Christians is the strong influence of the multiculturalism movement in public education. As this movement grows, it is not only removing from the curriculum many of the great works that have defined Western civilization but also often replacing them with books influenced by feminist and Marxist ideology.

Summary

For the Christian parent, choice takes on a much larger role. Like all other important decisions, schooling our children must depend on our understanding of what God would have us do as His servants. To choose wisely, we must know our children well and use discernment. What might be right for a child one school year might not work the next year. I believe that no single environment is appropriate for every child at every age. Each setting—public, private, and home education—has its benefits and weaknesses, and parents cannot assume that any educational setting is always the right one for their child. Choosing an educational setting can be as complex as our children.

We must also understand that a spiritual war is being fought for the minds and hearts of our children, and that the philosophy of this world is not compatible with the gospel of Jesus Christ. We have entered a period in our history as a nation when a biblical worldview is losing its influence. As a result, we must think carefully about the purpose of education. If education is only the accumulation of data or a place to be certified for employment, then almost any school will do. But if education is about determining what kind of people our children will become, then it is necessary to place greater importance on our educational choices.

In 1644, John Milton wrote a short essay on what education should accomplish for the Christian. It reads, in part, "The end then of learning is to repair the ruins of our first parents by regaining to know God aright, and out of that knowledge to love him, to imitate him, to be like him."[14] Are our children learning to become disciples of Christ and to love God with all of their hearts, their souls, and their minds?

12

Education Reform

Don Closson

I t's the end of your child's first semester of high school,
and you are expecting the usual report card. Instead,
he brings home a portfolio of work that exemplifies his
progress toward achieving a series of educational goals
established by the district. What are you to think?

Perhaps you have just found out that next year your
first grader will be attending a multiaged classroom that
uses a cooperative education format and a whole language,
interdisciplinary curriculum. What should you do?

What if you found out that your fifth-grade daughter
attends a school that endorses mastery learning, site-based
management, and an effective school administrative plan?
Is it time to panic?

In such circumstances, what is the proper course of
action? Should you pull your children out and homeschool
them? Should you enroll them in a private school? Or
should you be supportive of these new educational reforms?

Education reform, which seems to be never ending,
often places Christians in a difficult position. Frequently
it's hard to know which reforms are hostile to Christian
truth, which reforms are merely poorly conceived ideas,
and which reforms are actually worthwhile changes in the
way we educate children. Many Americans, Christian and

otherwise, are becoming cynical about education reform. Every new innovation promises to revolutionize the classroom, yet things seem to get progressively worse. The last decade has brought more sweeping reform to our schools than ever before, yet few people are convinced that our elementary and secondary schools are performing as we would like.

In this chapter, we evaluate the notion of education reform in America's public schools. First, we consider how one might evaluate reforms in general, and then we look at specific reforms that are currently being debated. These debates often center on five concerns, or what some people call crises, in our schools: the crisis of authority, the crisis of content, the crisis of methodology, the crisis of values, and the crisis of funding. The term *crisis* is used here to mean "a turning point" rather than "collapse or abandonment." Although your local school district might not be embroiled in all five of these concerns, each of them is widespread throughout the country.

Never have so many Americans been so unsure of their public schools, and many of these people are looking for answers, any answers, that will solve the problems that they think are destroying the effectiveness of education in America. This time of crisis coincides with a split in our society over some very basic notions of what America should be and on what intellectual and moral foundations its institutions should rest. This situation makes our response to these crises as Christians even more significant. It is also a time of opportunity for Christians to have considerable impact on the way our schools operate.

Although the terminology surrounding these crises can be esoteric, they are anything but ivory tower issues. Not only is a great deal of money (literally billions of tax dollars) involved but also how our children or perhaps our neighbor's children will be educated will be determined by the resolution of these issues.

Each crisis also represents an opportunity for the Christian community to be salt and light. To act as a preservative, we must be a discerning people. Too often, the Christian community responds to societal change with anger or passivity when neither reaction is appropriate. Once we gain an understanding of what is happening to our schools, we should respond in a biblically informed manner that seeks the best for both our own children and those of our community.

How to Evaluate Reform

Your local school district has just announced that it is installing a new grade school curriculum based on the most recent innovations from brain research. The staff touts the program as widely implemented and research based. As a parent, you have yet to take a position on the program, waiting until you have more information, but you feel at a loss as to what type of questions might be appropriate to ask to begin your evaluation.

The first step is to understand what is meant by a research-based innovation. For a school program to be truly research based, an incredible amount of effort must be invested. Unfortunately, few educational reforms are based on such foundations. Two professors of education, Arthur Ellis and Jeffrey Fouts at Seattle Pacific University, have written a book titled *Research on Educational Innovations* that offers some realistic guidelines for evaluation.[1] The first step in evaluating any reform is to realize that "Theories of human behavior have real, lasting consequences when we try them out on human beings."[2]

For that reason alone, we should be careful when applying theory to our classrooms.

Actually, three levels of research must be finished before proponents of a theory can claim that their curriculum or innovation is truly "research based." The first level is what might be called "pure research." This often consists of medical or psychological discoveries from clinical experimentation. This kind of research is most effective when it is specific in focus and highly controlled in methodology, but it might also be the result of philosophical inquiry. The thinking and writing of Jean Piaget on the development of the intellect is an example of a theoretical source for educational reform that was derived from both observation and philosophical speculation. Unfortunately, this is where the research support of many programs ends, but to be called research based much more must be done.

The second level of research involves testing and measuring a theory's implications for actual learning. Here, the theory discovered in the laboratory or in the minds of philosophers must be implemented in a classroom setting. With the help of carefully controlled groups, researchers can determine whether the innovation actually aids in achieving stated educational goals—that kids really do learn more. A third level of research requires educators to discern if this innovation can be applied successfully in diverse schoolwide settings.

To complete research on an innovation at these three levels takes time, money, and tenacity, three things that are often lacking in our schools. With the incredible political and social pressures to fix the system, educators often turn to programs that make dramatic promises yet lack the necessary testing and trial periods to substantiate the claims of their promoters.

For the Christian parent, establishing whether an educational reform is adequately researched is just the beginning of the evaluation process. Even if a program works in the sense that it achieves its stated goals, not all goals are equally desirable. Every reform must be weighed against biblical truth because reformers often make assumptions about human nature, morality, or other faith issues. Christian parents can never sit on the sidelines regarding their children's educational experiences because education, in all of its many facets, helps to shape our children's view of what is real and important in life.

Current Reforms

Outcome-based education (OBE) reform is causing some very heated debates throughout the country. At its core, OBE is a fairly simple framework around which a curriculum may be organized. It shifts schools away from the current focus on inputs to outcomes, from time units to measured abilities. It assumes that all kids can learn but not at the same speed. Instead of having all students take U.S. history for two semesters of sixteen weeks each, students would be given credit when they master a list of expected behavioral and cognitive outcomes. Not all students will complete the objectives at the same time. The focus is on the tasks to be accomplished, not the time it takes to accomplish them.

OBE would not qualify as a research-based innovation. It claims little or no research at the basic or primary level. At the classroom level, much of the associated research has been done on the concept of mastery learning. A considerable amount of work has been done on this teaching method, and many people think that it is a good thing. Others, such as Robert Slavin, argue that mastery learning produces limited or short-term results. This still leaves much of the OBE system without a research base. Level-three research, which seeks to determine if a reform innovation actually works at the district or school level, is mostly anecdotal. Stories of how districts have been turned around by OBE are rarely published in journals for critical review.

This doesn't mean that OBE is without merit; the point is that we really don't know. What most people get upset about is how some people in the educational bureaucracy have used OBE to establish a somewhat politically correct agenda as educational outcomes, often dealing more with feelings and attitudes than with knowledge and skills.

Another reform that creates conflict is the implementation of thinking skills programs. The idea is to formulate content-neutral classroom exercises that will enhance thinking skills across the curriculum. This idea assumes that certain skills can be isolated from content and taught to students. Unfortunately, there is no agreed-upon list of skills that should be included. Brain research, cognitive science, and information processing theories are possible sources for such a list, but according to Ellis and Fouts in their book *Research on Educational Innovations,* these theories have not been tied to basic research programs yet. Because of ambiguities at the basic level, little level-two research has been done to decide if learning can indeed be effected. One study done in 1985 (Norris) concluded that we don't know much about critical thinking and that what we do know suggests that it tends to be context sensitive, which strongly argues against the entire notion of thinking skills courses.

School- or district-wide studies of these thinking skills programs tend to consist of "success stories" with little analysis. Again, at this point there is very little evidence that thinking skills can be taught independently of content.

Both outcome-based reform and higher reasoning skills programs are examples of ideas that have found great favor among educators but little support among Christian parents. This situation often reflects the imposition by some educators of naturalistic or pantheistic assumptions via these reforms rather than a critical evaluation of the reform methods themselves. Unfortunately, some Christians have resorted to personal attacks on the reformers' motives rather than a careful study of the innovation or methodology itself.

Some school reforms are questionable from the beginning, comprehensive sex education being one that comes to mind. But other reforms might contain helpful attributes and yet be poorly implemented or grow into a dogma that drives out other good or necessary parts of the curriculum. Cooperative education and whole language programs often fit this description.

The two methodologies are different in that cooperative education has a well-established research base supporting it whereas whole language lacks much beyond level one or basic research. Christians have generally been against both concepts but for different reasons. Let's first describe the innovations themselves.

Cooperative education grew out of Kurt Lewin's research in the 1930s on group dynamics and social interaction. One description offered by an advocate states that "cooperative learning methods share the idea that students work together to learn and are responsible for one another's learning as well as their own." The idea is to use group motivation to get individuals to excel and grow. Most models of cooperative learning programs stress the following features:

- interdependence of learners
- student interaction and communication
- individual accountability
- instruction on social skills
- group processing of goal achievement

Some Christians have charged advocates of cooperative learning with wanting to do away with personal excellence and using group pressure to get children to conform to secular moral norms. I am sure that both of these complaints have justification, but this doesn't have to be the case. In fact, many advocates of cooperative learning don't want to do away with the competitive aspect of schooling, they just want to moderate it and to help students to develop the skill of working in groups. Working in groups does not conflict with Christian thinking. In fact, Christian schools and seminaries make use of similar techniques all of the time.

A problem occurs when over-zealous promoters of cooperative learning declare all competitive learning to be dangerous, or offer cooperative learning as a schooling panacea equivalent to a cure for cancer. Some teachers fail to hold students accountable for their work, which can lead to unequal effort and unjust rewards for individuals. This lesson damages student motivation and the integrity of the teacher.

Whole language has much less research to support its claims, most of which is at the theoretical or basic research level. Whole language theorists argue that language is acquired by actually using it rather than by learning its parts. It rejects the technical approach to language that encourages learning phonics and grammar rules rather than the simple joy of reading and writing. Unfortunately, there is little evidence that this approach teaches students to read and write well. A large study done in 1989 by Stahl and Miller concluded that there is no evidence that whole language instruction produces positive effects and that it might actually produce negative results.

This is not to say that some whole language ideas might not be implemented beneficially with the more traditional phonics, spelling, and grammar instruction. Its emphasis on reading actual literature, not basal readers, is a positive step, as is encouraging students to write often on diverse topics.

I have a number of problems from a theoretical viewpoint with what is promoted as whole language theory, but my response as a Christian should be to work with the teacher and the school my child attends or to find a setting that teaches in a manner that satisfies my expectations. In any case, a Christlike humility should pervade my contact with the teacher and school.

Educators Versus the Public

In spite of the fact that most Americans see the need for improving our public schools, there has been tremendous resistance to reform, both from parents and many teachers. Information found in a recent study titled *First Things First: What Americans Expect from the Public Schools* published by the Public Agenda Foundation might give us some reasons why.

Focusing on parents of public school children, and particularly on Christian and African-American families, the report found that these groups support most of the same solutions to our schools' problems. Both groups want higher educational standards and clear guidelines for what students should know and what teachers should teach.

They reject social promotions and overwhelmingly think that high school students should not graduate without writing and speaking English well. African-American parents were even more dissatisfied with their schools than others and are more concerned with low expectations on the part of educators.

A second finding was that school reform was viewed in fundamentally different ways by educators and the public. Most educators believe that schools are doing relatively well whereas the public thinks that much improvement is needed. In Connecticut, 68 percent of educators thought that the schools are better now than when they were in school. Only 16 percent of the public agreed. Educators and parents differ radically in their explanations for our schools' problems. Educators blame public complacency, taxpayer selfishness, and racism. Although the public supports integration and equal opportunity, it rejects the notion that more money will automatically fix our schools.

Parents' chief concerns are safe, orderly, and focused schools. Nine out of ten Americans believe that dependability and discipline will help our students learn better than reforms in test taking or assessments in general. Three out of four parents support permanently removing students caught with guns or drugs from our schools and temporarily removing those who misbehave. Unfortunately, educators rarely make these issues the center of reform proposals. Other findings include the belief that stable families are a more decisive factor for determining student success than is a particular school setting, and a perception that educators are often pushing untested experimental methods at the expense of the basics.

Educators and parents were also far apart on a number of classroom methods. Parents find nothing wrong with having kids memorize the fifty state capitals and where they are located or to learn to perform math functions without the aid of a calculator. Educators are much more likely to stress higher-order reasoning skills and the early use of calculators. Generally, parents are less preoccupied than educators with the need for sex education, AIDS education, multicultural experiences, and even school prayer.

There seems to be much common ground on which the vast majority of parents and other taxpayers agree. As Christians, we probably would be much happier with our schools if they were safe, orderly, and academically sound. Most Christian parents understand and accept the fact that their public schools will not be overtly Christian. But they also believe that the Christian faith and its presuppositions should receive fair treatment when reforms are instituted. In recent years, many Christian parents have seen their schools initiate programs that both challenge and ridicule their beliefs. This isn't necessary, and it has alienated the very people who must fund and support the schools if they are to be successful.

13

Multiculturalism

Don Closson

A few years ago, two professors published in the campus newspaper of a major university an essay titled *The Statement of the Black Faculty Caucus.*[1] The purpose of the essay was to define how the university might become a truly multicultural institution. It spoke of empowerment, authority, Western culture, and transformation. The objective of the Black Faculty Caucus was to create a critical mass of empowered "minority people" at all levels of the university system. The essay argued that "Euro-Americans teaching the materials of people of color cannot make the university multicultural because multiculturalism demands empowered people of color as well as empowered areas of knowledge."[2] At the end of their essay, the authors wrote, "What we are talking about here is no less than transforming the university into a center of multicultural learning: anything less continues a system of education that ultimately reproduces racism and racists."[3]

Racial reconciliation should be a top priority for all Christians, regardless of their racial or cultural background. But will this demand for a "multicultural center of learning" produce a less prejudiced society? Multiculturalists insist on greater sensitivity toward and increased inclusion of racial minorities and women in society. Christians should endorse both of these goals. But many people who are advocating multiculturalism go beyond these demands for sensitivity and inclusion; here is where Christians must be careful.

One of the difficulties of accommodating multiculturalists is that the definition of a multicultural society, curriculum, or institution seems to be determined by one's perspective. A commonly held view suggests that being multicultural involves tolerance toward racial and ethnic minorities, mainly in the areas of dress, language, food, religious beliefs, and other cultural manifestations. However, an influential group called the National Association for Multicultural Education (NAME) includes in its philosophy statement the following sentence: "Xenophobia, discrimination, racism, classism, sexism, and homophobia are societal phenomena that are inconsistent with the principles of a democracy and lead to the counterproductive reasoning that differences are deficiencies."[4] NAME is a powerful organization composed of educators from around the country, and it has considerable influence on how schools approach the issue of diversity on campus. The folks at NAME must answer this fundamental question: "Is it always counterproductive to reason that some differences might be deficiencies?" In other words, isn't it possible that some of the characteristics of specific culture groups are dangerous or morally flawed (e.g., the cultures of pedophilia and fascism)?

It is not uncommon for multiculturalism advocates such as NAME to begin with the assumption that truth is culturally based. It is argued that a group's language dictates which ideas about God, human nature, and morality are permissible. Whereas Americans might define reality by using principles from their Greek, Roman, and

Judeo-Christian heritage, Asian or African cultures see the world differently based on their traditions. Multiculturalists conclude that because multiple descriptions of reality exist, no single view can be true in any ultimate sense. Furthermore, because truth is a function of language and all language is created by humans, all truth is created by humans. Dr. Richard Rorty, humanities professor at the University of Virginia, is a spokesman for this view of truth and language. He argues that truth that transcends culture does not exist because "where there are no sentences there is no truth, and sentences and their respective languages are human creations."[5]

Finally, if all truth is created by humans, it is all equally true. Cultural ideas or institutions, like human sacrifice or welfare systems, are equally valid if they are useful for a given group of people. In other words, we live in a universe that is blind to moral choices. We are the final judges of how we shall live.

As Christians, we believe that ideas have consequences. While being careful not to promote one set of cultural rules over others simply because we are comfortable with them, we acknowledge that Scripture reveals to us the character and nature of God, humanity, and our need for a Savior. These truths can be communicated cross-culturally in a sensitive way, regardless of the people-group involved. If we do not believe this to be true universally, then Christianity cannot be true in any real way. To be what it claims to be, Christianity must transcend culture in a way that many multiculturalists argue is impossible.

Language and Sensitivity

In recent years, America has been attracting more than 1 million immigrants annually. This influx of foreigners has resulted in a country that is religiously, racially, and linguistically more diverse. Conflict arises, however, over the question of how our nation's institutions should respond to this diversity. Until recently, it was argued that America was a melting pot society, that regardless of an immigrant's origin, given a generation or two, the family would be assimilated into American culture. Multiculturalists have challenged both the reality and the advisability of this view.

Multiculturalists brand our culture as white, Western, male, Christian, middle class, and heterosexual. They declare that our schools have forced on students a curriculum that promotes only that perspective. The books students read, the ideas they consider, the moral and ethical standards they are taught, explicitly or implicitly, tend to be those of dead, white, European males. The problem, they argue, is that this tendency omits the contributions of many other people. The multiculturists' goal is to correct this bias against women, homosexuals, people of color, and people of various religious traditions who are ignored and thus silenced. This charge of bias is not totally groundless. Although many people think that Western culture has been very open to outside ideas, all majorities—in any society—will tend to seek cultural dominance.

The resulting multiculturalist agenda includes three demands on American society. The first demand is that the white Americans become more sensitive to minorities. This demand has resulted in what is referred to as "politically correct language." Speech codes enforcing sensitivity on college campuses have attempted to protect oppressed groups from having to endure words and ideas that might ostracize them. At the center of this issue is the individual's feelings or self-esteem. The multiculturalists argue that if a person's self-esteem is damaged, he or she cannot learn in school.

Christians ought to be the most sensitive people in society. If calling people handicapped, black, or Indian makes them feel diminished in importance or somehow less human, we as Christians need to be empathetic and make changes in our use of language. This sensitivity should arise from a sense of biblical humility, not from political or economic pressures.

Still another question must be answered. Will the enforced use (or prohibition) of certain words really benefit the self-esteem and thus the learning of minority students in schools, as some people have suggested? Dr. Paul Vitz, professor of psychology at New York University, argues that this is a far too simplistic view of human nature.[6] Self-esteem itself cannot be tied directly to any behavior, whether positive or negative.

Some people contend that enforcing "politically correct speech" is an attempt to redescribe our society in a manner that changes the way we think about issues. If the concepts of personal and family responsibility, for example, become labeled as "hate speech" toward welfare recipients, an entire way of looking at the issue is forced out of the dialogue.

Language can also be used to legitimize behavior that Christians believe to be morally wrong. Homosexuality progressively has been referred to as a sin, then as a disease, next as a lifestyle, and now as a sexual preference or orientation. Simply by redescribing this activity in new terms gives an entirely different connotation to what homosexuality is. This progression has not occurred by accident.

Hebrews 12:14 tells us to make every effort to be at peace with all people. As we articulate truth, our language should lean toward gentleness and respect for the sake of the gospel. When we believe that every person deserves to be respected because we are all created in the image of God, our attitudes will result in language and tones that are sensitive and gentle—not because political correctness demands it but because words of love flow from hearts of love.

Inclusion and Truth

A second demand being made on our schools and society is in the area of inclusiveness. Multiculturalists contend that marginalized people must be brought into the curriculum and the marketplace of ideas on campus. No group should ever have to feel left out. One example is the recent set of standards offered by the National Center for History in the Schools at the University of California at Los Angeles (UCLA). As originally offered, the standards greatly increased the voice of both minorities and women in the telling of our nation's history. However, many people charge that they denigrated or ignored the contributions of white Americans in the attempt to be inclusive. In fact, some people complained that the overall picture of America produced by the standards was of an oppressive, WASPish empire. Even the U.S. Senate denounced the proposed standards by a vote of 99 to 1. The sole dissenting senator voted against the resolution because it wasn't strong enough.

The standards declared that the United States is not a Western-based nation but the result of three cultures. The standards did not view these cultures—Native American, African-American, and European—as moral equals. In fact, the European contribution was presented as one of oppression, injustice, gender bias, and the rape of the natural world. Albert Shanker, president of the American Federation of Teachers, responded thus to the standards: "No other nation in the world teaches a national history that leaves its children feeling negative about their own country—this would be the first."[7]

American history textbooks have been moving toward inclusion for some time. To make up for the neglect of women and people of color in past texts, some historians and publishers have gone a bit overboard in their attempts at finding the right balance. In one text, *The American Nation,* only two of the thirteen religious leaders mentioned in short biographies are non-Hispanic white males (Brigham Young, one of the founders of Mormonism, and the transcendentalist Ralph Waldo Emerson).[8] Often women and minorities are injected oddly into the text. In this book, Senator Margaret Chase Smith is cited for challenging Senator Joseph McCarthy. Although she was an early critic of McCarthy, she had little to do with his eventual political demise. Another example is Native American chief George Crum, noted for making the first potato chips in 1853.[9]

The writing of history is a delicate task and is probably impossible to accomplish without bias. As Christians, we would prefer at least that truth—what *really* happened, rather than political or racial propaganda—be the goal, even if this goal will never be perfectly accomplished. (If all history is hopelessly political, including history written by ardent multiculturalists, then the entire enterprise is doomed!) This notion of truth demands that students be taught as much United States history from as many perspectives as possible. To leave out the experience of Native Americans, African-Americans, or women would be a tremendous failure. But writing our entire history from their perspective is also unfair.

One answer to this problem is to have students read more primary historical documents and depend less on history textbooks. Unfortunately, multiculturalists see all texts as primarily political. They argue that only one view prevails: either the empowered majority's view or the oppressed minority's view. This belief that all knowledge is political results in turning schools into battlegrounds where representatives from every group (Hispanics, African-Americans, feminists, and homosexuals) go over the curriculum with a magnifying glass, looking for the proper amount of inclusion or any derogatory remarks made about their group. For history to be meaningful, teachers and those who decide what will be taught in our schools must allow that historical evidence can be weighed, that interpretations of events can be right or wrong, and that we do get closer to an understanding of the real past when we read good works of history.[10]

Tolerance as a Worldview

Many multiculturalists insist that we embrace multiculturalism in our schools not only in the way we teach but also in the way we think. Multiculturalists have specific ideas about the notion of truth; paramount is the belief that no truth transcends culture, that no idea or moral concept is true for every cultural group or every human being. As a result, multiculturalists demand that we give up our belief in moral absolutes and become moral relativists.

This worldview model has been the litmus test for college professors on many campuses for quite some time, particularly in the humanities. Evidently, in some programs it is now being applied to college students as well.

In 1992, St. Cloud State University in Minnesota announced that if students were to be accepted, those who desired to enter the social work program must relinquish specific notions of moral truth.[11] Although the college acknowledged that many students come from religious backgrounds that do not accept homosexuality as a legitimate lifestyle, the college required these very students to go beyond "hating the sin and loving the sinner." Students who had predetermined negative attitudes toward gays and lesbians were told to look elsewhere for a major. In other words, to be admitted to this program, one must, at the level of faith commitment, find no moral aversion to homosexuality. This requirement immediately removes a majority of our population from consideration.

Part of the problem with multiculturalism is that it allows for a broad definition of cultural groups. There is both a gay culture and a feminist culture in America. In fact, any group can identify itself as a marginalized culture group. The homeless become a cultural group, as do single mothers on welfare. Should their perspectives get equal treatment in our schools? Are their moral values as valid as all others? The problem is that to be considered multiculturally sensitive, one must be able to place oneself completely into the perspective of the oppressed group at the metaphysical level, not just to sympathize or even empathize with them. This expectation means that one must be willing to compromise faith-based beliefs about God, human nature, and reality itself. For instance, if the gay community, being an oppressed minority group, believes that being homosexual is natural and every bit as normal as being heterosexual, Christians should ignore what they believe to be revealed truth about homosexuality's sinfulness.

Christians are called to have mercy and compassion on the poor and less fortunate, but not at the expense of recognizing that some lifestyles result in the impoverishment of people regardless of their race or cultural heritage. What Christians are being asked to do is to give up their view of a universe governed by a moral God who has established a moral universe and to replace it with a morally relativistic view. Tolerance becomes the only absolute. To be exclusive about truth, or to argue that some action might be morally wrong for all people all of the time, violates this new absolute of tolerance.

This current enforcement of tolerance is ultimately a thinly veiled pursuit of power. The only way that certain groups, such as homosexual activists or the more radical feminists, can get recognition and the ability to spread their views is by establishing tolerance as an absolute. Eventually, they win affirmative action concessions from universities and public schools, which enforce their viewpoint. Recently, Massachusetts passed legislation recognizing the difficulties of gay elementary and secondary students and forcing all public school teachers to be educated and sensitized to their plight. This recognition and re-education of teachers further legitimizes and enhances the power of the gay rights movement.

Christians must not lose sight of our calling to reach out and minister to people who are caught in lifestyles and cultures that vaunt themselves against the knowledge and standards of God; but we cannot become moral relativists in the process.

Justice and Truth

Although multiculturalists occasionally refer to justice, it cannot be the foundation of their movement simply because justice is not possible without truth. To claim that someone's actions or words are unjust, one must assume that a moral order really does exist, a moral order that would be true for all cultures and at all times. Injustice implies that justice exists, justice implies that moral laws exist, and moral laws imply that a lawgiver exists.

One college professor, explaining his plan for a liberal ironist utopia, says that a liberal is someone who thinks that being cruel is the worst thing that one can do. He argues that this moral standard can be used to create a utopia on earth. But he admits, being a good moral relativist, that he cannot give any noncircular arguments for why being cruel is the worst thing one can do. He is inventing a moral law, but he confesses that its foundation lies only in his preference for that law.[12]

Even if we accept the professor's moral standard as useful, it leaves us with many questions, the first of which is what it means to be cruel. Is it cruel to encourage people in their gay lifestyles given the short lifespan of male homosexuals, even without AIDS?[13] If pain is part of our definition of cruelty, should all operations be banned because, even if they are successful, pain might result? How can we know that being cruel is the worst thing one can do in a morally neutral universe? Without truth, without knowledge of right and wrong, justice is impossible, as is any notion of a good life. The word "cruel" becomes an empty word.

By declaring tolerance to be an absolute, multiculturalists are consistent with their view of reality. They see all human cultures as morally equal because of their faith in a naturalistic worldview. This view argues for a godless universe and recognizes chance as the only possible cause for what exists. If this is true, absolute tolerance is the best for which we can hope.

Christians, however, seek sensitivity and inclusion for a much better reason. We believe that every human being is created in God's image and reflects God's glory and majesty. We were created to have dominion over God's creation as His stewards; thus, we are to care for others because they are ultimately worthy of our care and concern. We are not to be cruel to others because the Creator of the universe made individuals to have fellowship with Him and He cares for them. This reasoning does not discount the fact that people are fallen and in rebellion against God. In fact, if we really care about people we will take seriously 2 Corinthians 5:19–20. First, God has made reconciliation with Him possible through His Son Jesus Christ and, ". . . he has committed to us the message of reconciliation. We are therefore Christ's ambassadors, as though God were making his appeal through us."

True sensitivity and inclusion will not be achieved by making tolerance an absolute. These occur when we take seriously both what people believe and the consequences of those beliefs. When you think about it, what could be crueler than failing to inform people of the gospel of redemption through Christ, thus leaving them to spend eternity separated from the Creator God who loves them?

14

Intellectual Capital

Don Closson

A recurring truth of education in America is that children from high-income homes who have highly educated parents tend to do well in school. Likewise, those from low-income homes who have relatively uneducated parents tend to do poorly. In this country, no other factor comes close to explaining the success of some students and the failure of others.[1] What is worse, recent studies are beginning to show that the gap between students from low socio-economic situations and their classmates is beginning to grow again after a period of narrowing.[2] Therefore, a major goal of education reform is the eradication of this learning gap, which is arguably the primary cause of continued poverty, high crime rates, and general distrust between those who participate in the American dream and those on its margins. Unfortunately, considerable disagreement exists as to how American public education should be reformed to accomplish this task.

Professional educators have tended to endorse a package of reforms that has been around since the 1920s and 1930s. These reforms are associated with the Progressive Education movement, which emphasized "naturalistic," "project-oriented," "hands-on," and "critical-thinking" curricula and "democratic" education policies.[3] Beginning in 1918 with the *Cardinal Principles of Secondary Education* published by the Bureau of Education, educators have challenged the emphasis on subject matter and have attempted to replace it with what might be called the "tool" metaphor.

The tool metaphor maintains that students should not be filled with a lot of useless knowledge; instead, they should be taught how to learn. Although various arguments are used to promote this view, the one most often heard goes something like this: "Because knowledge is growing so quickly—in fact, it is exploding—we must teach kids how to learn, not a bunch of facts that will quickly become outdated." Historian Lawrence Cremin has shown that our elementary schools have been dominated by this metaphor since the 1960s and that our secondary schools are not far behind.[4]

The result of the monopolized use of this metaphor has been a reduction of what might be called "intellectual capital." The loss of this capital is the focus of E. D. Hirsch's important book titled *The Schools We Need.* Hirsch is an advocate for what has been called "cultural literacy," the notion that all children need to be taught the core knowledge of our society to function within it successfully. Many people think that implementing his reforms might provide our only chance for equal opportunity for all Americans, regardless of class, race, or ethnicity.

For Christians, this is an issue of justice and mercy. Unless we are comfortable with the growing number of people who are unable to clothe, house, and feed themselves and their families, we must think seriously about why our educational system fails so many children. Teachers are paid more and have more education than ever before, and class sizes have declined significantly over the decades.

But while Americans spend much more to educate their children than do most other countries of the world, American students continue to fall behind in performance. Could it be that the problem lies in the philosophy that drives what teachers teach and how they teach it? Our argument is exactly that. Educators, particularly at the elementary level, have adopted a view of education that places an extra burden on those who can least afford it— our least affluent children.

Defining Intellectual Capital

Earlier, we stated that poverty and suffering in America can be blamed partially on an education system that fails to prepare children from lower socio-economic backgrounds with a foundation that will allow them to compete with children from middle- and upper-class homes. Central to this argument is a notion called intellectual capital.

In his book *The Schools We Need,* Hirsch argues that "just as it takes money to make money, it takes knowledge to make knowledge."[5] He contends that children who begin school with an adequate level of intellectual capital have a framework upon which further learning may be built. Children who lack the necessary educational experiences and sufficient vocabulary tend to fall farther and farther behind.

Not just any information serves as intellectual capital. According to Hirsch, the knowledge taught and learned must be of a type that "constitutes the shared intellectual currency of the society," or put another way, "intellectual capital has to be the widely useful and negotiable coin of the realm."[6] Just as play money doesn't purchase much in the real world, neither does knowledge that falls outside of this "shared intellectual currency." Time spent on

Ebonics, comic books as literature, or self-esteem exercises would not fit into Hirsch's notion of intellectual currency. Although of possible value, these topics would not help young people who must compete in the American economic system.

Understanding Hirsch's point about intellectual capital would be interesting although not very useful if not for the fact that research has shown that initial learning deficits in specific children can be overcome if addressed at an early age. Other nations, with equally diverse populations, have shown that early disparities in learning can be remediated if this notion of a shared knowledge base is taken seriously.

France is an example of such a nation. Its "knowledge intensive" early childhood education programs have performed an amazing feat. "Remarkably, in France, the initial gap between advantaged and disadvantaged students, instead of widening steadily as in the United States, decreases with each school grade. By the end of seventh grade, the child of a North African immigrant who has attended two years of French preschool will on average have narrowed the socially induced learning gap."[7]

One might ask what American schools are teaching if not a knowledge-intensive "core curriculum" like the one found in the French model. This question is difficult to answer because there is no agreed-upon curriculum for elementary students in this country. Our desire to treat teachers as autonomous teaching professionals often means that little or no supervision of what is taught occurs. A number of good arguments exist for local control of our schools, but when it comes to the curriculum, there has been little consistency from one school to another or even from one classroom to another in the same building.

Can't we all agree that by the end of the first grade students ought to be able to do and know certain things? Unfortunately, it's not that simple. At this point, we will look at some of the philosophical reasons for the vast difference in teaching methods and goals that are being advocated by different education experts.

Romantics and Traditionalists

In his book *The Schools We Need,* Hirsch argues that there are two distinct camps of education reformers in our country today. One group, which is virtually in control of the elementary and much of the secondary school curriculum, consists of what Hirsch calls the anti-knowledge progressives. This group emphasizes critical thinking skills over mere facts, the "unquestionable" value of self-esteem as a curricular end, and teaching "to the child" rather than from curriculum focused on the content of the subject matter. They also argue against forcing a child to learn what they believe to be developmentally inappropriate schoolwork. This thinking reflects the eighteenth-century Romantic view that all children possess a spark of divinity, a notion that coincides with the pantheistic philosophies of eighteenth-century thinkers such as Rousseau, Hegel, and Schelling. In 1775, Schelling wrote that "the God-infused natural world and human nature were both emanations of the same divine substance."[8] All things natural are good. Evil lies in separation from nature, such as seating children in rows and requiring intense study from books for several years.

Rather than allowing for a mystical view of child development, traditionalists support a "core curriculum." Hirsch points to four errors made by progressive reforms. He argues that: "(1) To stress critical thinking while de-emphasizing knowledge actually reduces a student's capacity to think critically. (2) Giving a child constant praise to bolster self-esteem regardless of academic achievement breeds complacency, or skepticism, or both, and ultimately, a decline in self-esteem. (3) For a teacher to pay significant attention to each individual child in a class of twenty to forty students means individual neglect for most children most of the time. (4) Schoolwork that has been called [by progressives] 'developmentally inappropriate' has proved to be highly appropriate to millions of students the world over, while the infantile pabulum now fed to American children is developmentally inappropriate (in a downward direction) and often bores them."[9]

As parents and taxpayers, the most vital question we want answered is, "Who is right?" Does research support one side of this debate over the other? Hirsch contends that there is much evidence, from various perspectives, that supports the traditional view. However, because of the current monopoly of the progressive mind-set in public education today, the traditional view is rarely even considered. Hirsch goes as far as to say that for most public school officials there is no thinkable alternative to the progressive view. "No professor at an American education school is going to advocate *pro*-rote-learning, *pro*-fact, or *pro*-verbal pedagogy."[10]

Education leaders usually respond in one of four ways to criticism:

1. They deny that our schools are ineffective.
2. They deny the dominance of progressivism itself.
3. They deny that where progressivism has been followed it has been authentically followed.
4. They blame insurmountable social problems on poor performance rather than on the prevailing educational philosophy.

Remember, this discussion is about more than which group of experts wins and which loses! If Hirsch is right, our current form of schooling is inflicting a great injustice on all students but even more so on those from our poorest homes and neighborhoods. Now we will look at some of the evidence that argues against the progressive approach to education and for a more traditional curriculum.

Looking at the Research

Research has confirmed the superiority of the traditional, direct instruction method, which focuses on the content to be learned rather than on the child. *The Schools We Need* has a chapter titled "Reality's Revenge" that lends considerable detail to his argument that progressive educational theory lacks a real world foundation.

Hirsch uses evidence from three different sources to support his rejection of the progressive model for instruction. Classroom studies, research in cognitive psychology, and international comparisons point to a common set of practices that promote the greatest amount of measurable learning by the largest number of students. This list of common practices is remarkable in that they are exactly what progressive educators in this country are arguing that we should do *less of*.

First, let's consider the findings of two examples of classroom studies. Jane Stallings studied 108 first-grade and fifty-eight third-grade classes taught by different methods and found that a strong academic focus rather than the project-method approach produced the highest gains in math and reading. The Brophy-Evertson studies on elementary students in the 1970s found that classroom teaching was most effective when it

1. focused on content,
2. involved all students,
3. maintained a brisk pace,
4. required students to read aloud often,
5. required mastery of decoding skills to the point of overlearning, and
6. asked each child to perform tasks resulting in immediate nonjudgmental feedback.

Summarizing the results of numerous classroom studies, Hirsch states, "The only truly general principle that seems to emerge from process-outcome research on pedagogy is that focused and guided instruction is far more effective than naturalistic, discovery, learn-at-your-own-pace instruction."[11]

Cognitive psychology confirms from another viewpoint what classroom research has already told us. Research into short-term memory has uncovered important reasons to have children in the early elementary years spend considerable effort memorizing language and mathematics basics. The argument is that individuals have only so much room, or short-term memory, in which to juggle a number of ideas at once, and this memory space is particularly restricted for young children. In reading, children end up having to focus on both the basics of decoding and word recognition as well as high-level comprehension strategies. This gives those who have memorized phonics and who have a larger vocabulary a significant advantage over those who haven't. Children who overlearn decoding and word skills have more time, as far as memory, to focus on higher-level thinking. In other words, rote memorization of the basics leads to higher-order thinking, which is exactly the opposite of what the progressives are emphasizing.

If Christians want to see our public schools become tools for social justice, to educate all children regardless of background, a content-oriented curriculum is essential. An early emphasis on higher-level thinking skills is not only a poor use of time in the classroom but also can actually retard students from disadvantaged backgrounds. This problem is particularly true of the early elementary years when decoding skills and a large vocabulary are being acquired.

International and Domestic Examples

In the discussion thus far, we have been trying to discern why much of what happens in many of our classrooms fails to provide the intellectual capital that elementary school children need. At this point, we should note and emphasize that we are not questioning the desire of our classroom teachers or those who write curricula for the classroom to benefit our children. We do argue, however, that the philosophical foundations for today's educational theories often are supported by neither research nor a biblical view of human nature.

Earlier we noted classroom studies and findings from cognitive psychology that refute progressive educational practices. Now we will see how international studies add more evidence to this argument for a content-focused curriculum.

International studies have found that the best American classrooms are those similar to Asian classrooms, business-like and focused on the job at hand. Chinese and Japanese teachers have a low tolerance for errors and rarely let self-esteem issues get in the way of correcting errors. In fact, they use these errors in assessing the strengths and weaknesses of various tactics for solving a problem. Asian classrooms begin a period with reciprocal bows and a description of what will be accomplished during the lesson. The period ends with a summary of the work. The pace tends to be slower than in American classrooms, but skills are taught with greater thoroughness. Fewer problems are covered with the focus on mastering them rather than simply getting them done.

Asian teachers tend to use whole-class instruction, using students' responses to generate dialogue that moves the class toward the desired knowledge or skill. Students know that they may be called upon at any moment to provide a solution to the problem at hand. They are engaged and focused on the material. During the period, students might work together in groups on a problem but only for a short time. Asian teachers assign less seat work to their students and embed it throughout a lesson rather than at the end of class. The American practice of giving students a long block of time at the end of class to do homework usually causes students to lose focus and become bored with the repetitive tasks.

To achieve the greatest results, the classroom must be content oriented, and the teacher must be working hard to keep all of the students engaged in the work. Too often, American classrooms lack one of these two essential ingredients.

Hirsch's proposals, although revolutionary to many of today's teachers, would seem obvious to most teachers of a generation ago. They are also obvious to many Christian educators. A good example is the classical Christian education model advocated by Douglas Wilson and his Logos Schools organization.[12] Wilson endorses the *Trivium* curriculum model, which focuses on grammar in the early grades; dialectic, or logic, in the middle school; and rhetoric in the high school. Grammar is the memorization of the basic rules and facts of any subject matter, whether it be language or mathematics. The dialectic stage teaches students how the rules of logic apply to a subject area, and rhetoric teaches students how to communicate what they have learned. All of this can be done such as to make it both challenging and meaningful to the vast majority of public and private school students. However, if we fail to accomplish this soon, we will continue to see a widening gap between those who have been vested with intellectual capital and those who have not.

15

Outcome-Based Education

Don Closson

The decade of the 1980s brought about numerous education reforms, but few of them were a dramatic shift from the past. A new, even revolutionary type of reform called outcome-based education (OBE) found favor near the end of the decade and has often been promoted as the panacea for America's educational woes. Although components of OBE have been around for decades, if implemented, this approach to curriculum development could change our schools more than any other recent reform proposal. Originally motivated by demands for greater accountability of how our education dollars are spent (a politically conservative ideal), it has been adopted by those who think that it is a perfect tool for breaking with traditional ideas about how and what we teach our children (a progressive ideal).

The focus of past and present curriculum has been on content, the knowledge to be acquired by each student. Our language, literature, history, customs, traditions, and morals—often called Western civilization—dominated the learning process through secondary school. If students learned the information and performed well on tests and assignments, they received credit for the course and moved on to the next class. The point here is that the curriculum centered on the content to be learned; its purpose was to produce academically competent students. The daily school routine was organized around this academic content, which was organized into subject areas. Each hour was devoted to a teacher's delivering information on a given topic; some students responded well to the instruction, and some did not.

Outcome-based education proposes to change the focus of schools from the content to the student. According to William Spady, a major advocate of this type of reform, three goals drive this new approach to creating school curricula. First, all students can learn and succeed but not on the same day or in the same way. Second, each success by a student breeds more success. Third, schools control the conditions of success.[1] In other words, students are assumed to be very malleable creatures. If we create the right environment, any student can be prepared for any academic or vocational career. The key is to custom fit classrooms to each student's learning style and abilities.

The resulting schools will be vastly different from the ones that recent generations attended. Yearly and daily schedules will change, teaching responsibilities will change, classroom activities will change, the evaluation of student performance will change and, most importantly, our perception of what it means to be an educated person will change.

What Is OBE?

Education is a political and emotional process. Pennsylvania, Florida, North Carolina, and Kansas have been rocked by political battles over the implementation of OBE reforms. Governors, legislators, state boards of education, and parents have been wrestling over how—and even if—

this reform should reshape our schools. Twenty-six other states claim to have generated outcome-based programs, and at least another nine more states are moving in that direction.[2]

Before considering the details of this controversy, let's review the major differences between the traditional approach to schooling in America and an outcome-based approach.

Whereas previously the school calendar determined what a child might do at any moment of any school day, now progress toward specific outcomes will control activity. Time, content, and teaching technique will be altered to fit the needs of *each* student. Credit will be given for accomplishing stated outcomes, not for time spent in a given class.

The teacher's role in the classroom will become that of a coach. The instructor's goal is to move each child toward predetermined outcomes rather than to attempt to transmit the content of Western civilization to the next generation in a scholarly fashion. This dramatic change in the role of the teacher will occur because the focus is no longer on content. Feelings, attitudes, and skills such as learning to work together in groups will become just as important as learning information—some reformers would argue that it will become *more* important. Where traditional curricula focused on the past, reformers argue that outcome-based methods prepare students for the future and the constant change that is inevitable in our society.

Many advocates of OBE think that evaluation methods must change as well because outcomes are now central to curriculum development. We can no longer rely on simple cognitive tests to determine complex outcomes. Vermont is testing a portfolio approach to evaluation in which works of art, literary works, and the results of group projects are added to traditional tests to evaluate a student's progress. Where traditional testing tended to compare the abilities of students with each other, outcome-based reform will be criterion based, meaning that all students must master information and skills at a predetermined level before they can move on to the next unit of material.

Implementing OBE Reform

Reformers advocating an outcome-based approach to curriculum development point to the logical simplicity of its technique. First, a list of desired outcomes in the form of student behaviors, skills, attitudes, and abilities is created. Second, learning experiences are designed that will allow teachers to coach the students to a mastery level in each outcome. Third, students are tested. Those who fail to achieve mastery receive remediation or retraining until mastery is achieved. Fourth, upon completion of the prescribed learner outcomes, a student graduates.

On the surface, this seems to be a reasonable approach to learning. In fact, the business world has made extensive use of this method for years, specifically for skills that were easily broken down into distinct units of information or specific behaviors. But as a comprehensive system for educating young minds, a few important questions have been raised, the most obvious of which is who will determine the specific outcomes or learner objectives. This is also the area that is creating the most controversy across the country.

Traditional Versus Transformational Outcome-Based Education

According to William Spady, a reform advocate, outcomes can be written with traditional, transitional, or transformational goals in mind. Spady advocates transformational goals, but let's consider traditional programs first.

Traditional outcome-based programs would use the new methodology to teach traditional content areas such as math, history, and science. Illinois is an example of a state that uses this approach. Although outcomes drive the schooling of Illinois children, the outcomes themselves reflect the traditional content of public schools in the past.

Many teachers find this a positive option for challenging the minimal achiever. For example, a considerable number of students currently find their way through our schools, accumulating enough credits to graduate but picking up little in the way of content knowledge or skills. Their knowledge base reflects little actual learning, but they have become skilled in working the system. An outcome-based program would prevent such students from graduating or passing to the next grade without reaching a preset mastery level of competency.

The idea of transformational reform is causing much turmoil. Transformational OBE subordinates course content to key issues, concepts, and processes. Indeed, Spady calls this the "highest evolution of the OBE concept."[3] Central to the idea of transformational reform is the notion of outcomes of significance. Examples of such outcomes from Colorado and Wyoming school systems refer to collaborative workers, quality producers, involved citizens, self-directed achievers, and adaptable problem solvers. Spady supports transformational outcomes because they are future oriented, based on descriptions of future conditions that he thinks should serve as starting points for OBE designs.

True to the spirit of the reform philosophy, little mention is made about specific things that students should know as a result of being in school. The focus is on attitudes and feelings, personal goals, initiative, and vision—in the advocates' words, the whole student.

It is in devising learner outcomes that one's worldview comes into play. Those who see the world in terms of constant political and moral change find a transformational model useful. They view human nature as evolving and changing rather than fixed.

Christians, however, see human nature as fixed and unchanging. Although we were created in God's image, we are now fallen and sinful. We also hold to moral absolutes based on the character of God. The learner outcomes that have been proposed are controversial because they often accept a transformational, changing view of human nature. Advocates of OBE point with pride to its focus on the student rather than on course content. They think that the key to education reform is to be found in having students master stated learner outcomes. Critics fear that this is exactly what will happen. Their fear is based on the desire of reformers to educate the whole child. What will happen, they ask, when stated learner outcomes violate the moral or religious views of parents?

For example, most sex-education courses used in our schools claim to take a value-neutral approach to human sexuality. Following the example of the Kinsey studies and materials from the Sex Education and Information Council of the United States, most curricula make few distinctions between various sex acts. Sex within marriage between those of the opposite sex is not morally different from sex outside of marriage between those of the same sex. The goal of such programs is self-actualization and making people comfortable with their sexual preferences.

Under the traditional system of course credits, a student could take a sex-education course, totally disagree with the instruction, and yet pass the course by doing acceptable work on the tests presented. Occasionally, an instructor might make life difficult for a student who fails to conform, but if the student learns the material that would qualify him or her for a passing grade and credit toward graduation, he or she is promoted or graduated.

If transformational outcome-based reformers have their way, such a student would not get credit for the course until his or her attitudes, feelings, and behaviors match the desired goals of the learner outcomes. In Pennsylvania, for instance, the state board of education had recommended learner outcomes that would evaluate a student based on his or her ability to demonstrate a comprehensive understanding of families. Many people believe that this learner outcome is part of the effort to widen the definition of families to include homosexual couples. Another goal requires students to know about and *use* community health resources.[4] Notice that just *knowing* that Planned Parenthood has an office in town isn't enough; one must *use* it.

Parents Versus the State

The point of this discussion is to say that transformational outcome-based reform would be a much more efficient mechanism for changing our children's values and attitudes about issues facing our society. Unfortunately, the direction that these changes often take is in conflict with our Christian faith. At the core of this debate is the question of who has authority over the nation's children. Public officials often assume that they do. Governor Robert Casey of Pennsylvania, calling for reform, told his legislature, "We must never forget that you and I—the elected representatives of the people—and not anyone else—have the ultimate responsibility to assure the future of our children."[5] I hope that this statement is merely political hyperbole. I would argue that the *parents* of the children in the state of Pennsylvania are ultimately responsible for their children's future. The state has rarely proved itself to be a trustworthy parent.

Outcome-based education is an ideologically neutral tool for curricular construction; whether it is more effective than traditional approaches remains to be seen. Unfortunately, because of its student-centered approach, its ability to influence individuals with a politically correct set of doctrines seems to be great. Parents (and all other taxpayers) must weigh the possible benefits of outcome-based reform against its potential negative consequences.

Other Concerns About Outcome-Based Education

Many parents are concerned about who will determine the learner outcomes for their schools. One criticism already being heard is that many states have adopted very similar outcomes regardless of the process put in place to get community input. Many people wonder if there will be real consideration of what learner outcomes the public wants or if officials will assume that educators know what's best for our children. Who will decide what it means to be an educated person—the tax-paying consumer or the providers of education?

If students are going to be allowed to proceed through the material at their own pace, what happens to the brighter children? Eventually, students will be at many levels. What then? Will more teachers be necessary? Will computer-assisted instruction allow for individual learning speeds? Either option will cost more money. Some reformers offer a scenario in which brighter students help tutor slower students, thereby encouraging group responsibility rather than promoting an elite group of learners. Critics think that a mastery-learning approach will inevitably hold back brighter students.

Along with outcome-based reform, many educators are calling for a broader set of evaluation techniques. Attempts at grading students based on portfolios of various kinds of works have proved difficult. The Rand Corporation studied Vermont's attempt and found that "rater reliability—the extent to which raters agreed on the quality of a student's work—was low."[6] There is a general dislike of standardized tests among the reformers because these focus on what the child knows rather than on the whole child. But is there a viable substitute? Will students find that it is more important to be politically correct than to know specific facts?

Another question that reformers must answer is whether school bureaucracies will allow for such dramatic change. How will the unions respond? Will legislative mandates that are already on the books be removed, or will this new approach simply be laid over the rest, creating a jungle of regulations and red tape? Reformers supporting OBE claim that local schools will actually have more control over their programs. Once learner outcomes are established, schools will be given the freedom to create programs that accomplish these goals. But critics respond by noting that although districts might be given input as to how these outcomes are achieved, local control of the outcomes themselves will be lost.

Finally, many people think that focusing on transformational learner outcomes will allow for hidden agendas to be promoted in the schools. Many parents think that there is already too much emphasis on global citizenship, radical environmentalism, humanistic views of self-esteem, and human sexuality at the expense of reading, writing, math, and science. They think that education will become more propagandistic than academic in nature. Parents should learn where their state is in regard to this movement. If an outcome-based program is being pursued, will it focus on traditional or transformational outcomes? If the outcomes are already written and adopted, can a copy be obtained? If they are not yet written, how can parents get involved?

If a state is considering a transformational OBE program, parental concerns should be brought before the legislature. If the reform is local, parents should contact their school board. Parents have an obligation to know what is being taught to their children and if it works. Recently, parental resistance halted the OBE movement in Pennsylvania when parents pointed out to the legislature that there is no solid evidence that the radical changes proposed will actually cause kids to learn more. Although a new movement among school administrators stresses the importance of parental input and support for reforms, only watchful diligence will guarantee that our children do not suffer from whatever the current educational fad might be.

16

Self-Esteem Curricula

Don Closson

The use of self-esteem curricula in our schools has been a point of contention with Christians for the last twenty years. Educators claim that focusing on positive self-esteem can encourage creativity, increase concentration, decrease drug use, and delay sexual activity. Often called life-skills programs, self-esteem materials have been incorporated into programs for gifted students, sex education, drug education, and regular classrooms in both public and private schools. Although many self-esteem-oriented programs are now used in schools, Quest, Pumsy, DUSO (Developing Understanding of Self and Others), and DARE (Drug Abuse Resistance Education) have had remarkable success.

Opponents of the programs argue that the focus on self-esteem is a direct result of a change in the way we view human nature. This change has influenced our society in a number of ways. God has been replaced by humanity as the center of knowledge and ethics. The result has been movement toward a relativistic view of morality that discourages belief in transcendent moral values. Students are told to seek truth within and to see their moral values and personal ethics as a by-product of that process. This approach has resulted in the view that truth is relative and bio-graphical; what is true for you might not be true for me.

The year 1986 is often looked upon as the birth of the self-esteem movement in America. California sponsored a study on self-esteem called the *California Task Force to Promote Self-Esteem and Personal and Social Responsibility.* The driving force behind the legislation was California State Assembly member John Vasconcellos. His personal search for self-esteem sheds light on the nature of this move-ment. Vasconcellos was raised in a strict Catholic home. He writes, "I had been conditioned to know myself basi-cally as a sinner, guilt ridden and ashamed, constantly beating my breast and professing my unworthiness."[1] But in the 1960s, he went through a period of Rogerian person-centered therapy with a priest/psychologist and claims that he became more fully integrated and more whole. Thus, he turned his lifework toward promoting self-esteem.

Vasconcellos sees two possible models for defining human nature. The first he labels a constrained vision, supported by the writings of Adam Smith, Thomas Hobbes, and Frederick Hayek. The second model is an unconstrained vision, associated with Jean-Jacques Rousseau and John Locke. The constrained vision sees humanity as basically evil, needing to be governed and controlled. The unconstrained vision, however, sees hu-manity as basically good and possibly perfectible. After hearing Carl Rogers speak on the subject, Vasconcellos chose the second view. He argues that the self-esteem movement is built upon the "faith that people are basically good and that a relationship exists between self-esteem and healthy human behavior." He adds that self-esteem is a "deeply felt appreciation of 'oneself and one's natural being,' a trust of one's instincts and abilities."[2]

This background information about Vasconcellos is important for understanding why this controversy is so heated and significant. It is about not only what curricula will be used to teach our children but also about how we view human nature itself. Our view of human nature will determine the kind of education we design for our children and the goals to which education will aspire.

Visualization and Self-Esteem

Vasconcellos believes that self-esteem results from developing a deeply felt appreciation of oneself and one's natural being. But what is our natural being? Some people who hold to an Eastern view of human nature have argued that our natural being is spiritual and ultimately one with the rest of the universe.

A subtle example of this view is a curriculum written by Lorraine Plum called "Flights of Fantasy." The manual says,

> "Flights of Fantasy" is designed to enhance and refine children's natural inclination to image and fantasize—to use this special ability as a powerful vehicle for developing language, creativity, relaxation and a positive self-concept.

It adds that

> . . . only when we consciously and consistently provide experiences that acknowledge the body, the feelings, and the spirit, and honor both hemispheric functions of the brain, can we say with any sense of integrity that we are striving to develop the whole person.[3]

Just what is meant by providing experiences that acknowledge a person's spirit? Plum argues that two types of seeing are available to us. The first type is "external seeing," a combination of optical sensory abilities and the interpreting ability of the brain. The other type is "internal seeing," which uses the brain's ability to visualize or fantasize. Plum believes that each type of seeing is real in the sense that our bodies respond equally to both. Finally—and here's the pitch for an Eastern view of human nature—Plum asserts that, with its visualization and fantasy experiences, "Flights of Fantasy" will help students feel connected to nature and the entire universe, be more open to risk-taking, develop a sense of wonder, and become aware of personal power. All of these notions fit well into an Eastern, New Age perspective.

According to New Age teachers, distinctions in the physical realm are mere illusions. When we get in touch with our oneness with all that exists, we will have inner powers similar to Christ and other so-called risen masters. In a sense, humans are gods, though limited, who suffer from amnesia. A consciousness-raising experience is necessary to reconnect with this oneness. At this point, various meditative states, visualization techniques, and yoga are used to break through our Enlightenment Rationalism and experience oneness with all that exists.

Not every instructor using these materials buys into this religious view. Many teachers use them innocently, hoping to bring experiences into their classroom that might somehow benefit troubled students. But some authors (such as Jack Canfield, author of the "Chicken Soup" series and a friend of John Vasconcellos) have a definite purpose in mind. In his article "Education in the

New Age," Canfield promotes activities that put children in contact with wisdom that he believes lies deep within each of us. He sees himself as a bridge between Eastern and Western thought, particularly in our schools.[4]

At a minimum, "Flights of Fantasy" gives the impression that people can change their psychological state by sheer self-will. The manual states,

> If we visualize ourselves as being unsuccessful, we will be . . . If the images are portraits of self-doubt and failure, we have the power to replace them with self-confident, successful images. If we are unable to get into the image mentally, we will not get into the behavior physically.[5]

This view of human nature omits any notion of sin or an obligation to a transcendent moral order. It views humans as perfectible, self-correcting, autonomous beings. This curriculum opens the door to an Eastern view of human nature, one that conflicts dramatically with the biblical view that we are the creation of a personal, all-powerful, loving God.

Pumsy

A very popular theme of modern culture is the concept of "wisdom within." The heroes in George Lucas's *Star Wars* movies look inward to use the power of "The Force," and Shirley MacClaine's New Age gospel teaches that we must turn inward to find truth. Pumsy, a self-esteem curriculum used in primary schools across the country, focuses on this "wisdom within" theme. Although Pumsy teaches many behaviors that Christians can wholeheartedly endorse and attempts to help children be independent from peer influence, it also teaches subtly that children have an autonomous source of wisdom within themselves.

Advocates of self-esteem curricula argue that these programs are necessary to help children who are over-whelmed by a negative peer group or home environment, but they also claim that all children can benefit from class time spent focusing within themselves and being told how naturally good they are. It assumes that if children get in touch with their natural goodness, they will automatically behave in a manner that is personally rewarding. *Physician* magazine has challenged this notion that all children would benefit by the counsel provided by such a curriculum. It stated,

> No need for such broad-based, unselected intervention counseling has ever been sci-entifically established. In fact, government studies have shown that 87 percent of chil-dren do not need the emotional and behav-ioral "help" that programs like Pumsy claimed to provide. The net effect, there-fore, is potentially very harmful to a major-ity of elementary students.[6]

If a majority of our students do not need this type of therapy, why take away valuable time from academic pursuits?

Pumsy is the name of an imaginary dragon. When she is in her clear mind, she feels good about herself; when she is in her mud mind, nothing goes right—she doesn't like herself or anything else. Students are told that they, too, have this clear/mud mind dilemma and that they can leave behind their mud minds and put on a clear mind whenever they choose. In other words, bad feelings can be overcome merely by choosing to ignore them and by positing a clear mind.

Songs that the children sing focus on the same theme. The lyrics to one such song are, "I am special. So are you. I am enough. You are, too." Another song says, "When I am responsible for my day, many, many things seem to go my way. Good consequences. Good consequences. That's the life for me!"[7] The message of this curriculum is not very subtle. Humans have the power to perfect themselves emotionally and psychologically; they need only to choose to do so. The only sin that exists is not choosing a clear mind.

This curriculum prompts some important questions. Are all negative feelings bad? Is it necessarily a good thing to be able to shut off mourning for a lost loved one? Can a person really alter his or her situation merely by thinking positively? We all recognize the importance of self-confidence, but how closely does the self-esteem taught by this program match reality? Does it really benefit our students? When we read that American students perform poorly on international math tests yet feel good about their ability to do math, something is wrong.[8] Could we be causing students to develop a false security based on feelings that might not match reality? From a Christian viewpoint, our children need to know that they bear God's image, which bestows great dignity and purpose to life. They must also be made aware of the reality of sin and the fact that they are fallen creatures in need of redemption, transformation, and a renewal of their minds to be more like Christ.

Quest

Quest is one of the most used drug-education programs in America. It includes high school, junior high, and some grade school components. What makes discussion of this curriculum difficult is that its founder, Rick Little, is a Christian who used input from other Christians in its development.

In its original form, the program used values-clarification and other nondirective techniques, visualization exercises, and moral decision-making models. These methods have not proven successful in reducing drug use and have been accused of promoting a value-relative worldview.[9] Howard Kirschenbaum, who is closely associated with the values clarification movement of the 1970s, was hired to write the original curriculum and directed the program toward this approach. Quest makes some of the same assumptions about human nature as Pumsy. If students get in touch with their true selves—which are, by nature, good—they will not do drugs or be sexually active at an early age. If they see their true value, they will choose only healthy options. The key, according to Quest authors, is not to preach or be highly directive to the kids. Teachers are to be facilitators of discussion, not builders of character. The students naturally determine what is right for them via the decision-making model presented in class. Once they arrive at the right values, Quest assumes that they will live consistently with them. The presumptions are that humans desire to do what is right once the right thing is determined and that they can do so by using their own moral convictions.

To be fair, some of the more blatant values-clarification and visualization techniques have been removed, and Kirschenbaum is no longer part of the program. But many people still find the overall emphasis to be nondirective and morally relativistic. Ken Greene, an executive director who left the company in 1982, said,

We thought we were doing God's will and
had invested tremendous amounts of energy
and time. . . . It still leaves me a little
confused. I sometimes say, "Lord, did we
forsake the cross?"[10]

James Dobson, a contributor to the original Quest
textbook, recently voiced his concerns about parts of the
program. Although he notes that the curriculum has positive aspects, he adds that the authors have incorporated
the work of secular humanists into the curriculum and
have prescribed group exercises and techniques closely re-
sembling those employed in psychotherapy. This, he argues, is a "risky practice in the absence of professionally
trained leadership."[11] According to William Kilpatrick,
an education professor at the University of Boston,

Despite its attempts to distance itself from
its past . . . Quest remains a feelings-based
program. It still operates on the dubious assumption that morality is a by-product of
feeling good about yourself, and it still ad-
vertises itself as a child-centered approach.[12]

As was mentioned earlier, affective-oriented drug-
education programs do not have a good track record. In
1976, researcher Richard Blum found that an "affective
drug program" called "Decide" had little positive effect
on drug use. Those who sat in the class actually used more
drugs than a control group. He found similar results in a
repeat of the study in 1978. Research was conducted on
other affective programs in the 1980s. "Smart," "Here's
Looking at You," and Quest were found to increase drug
use rather than reduce it.[13] Before newer editions came out,

a number of states removed Quest from their approved drug-education list because it failed to comply with federal mandates that programs clearly state that drugs are harmful and against the law.

Criticism and an Alternative

Although an early advocate of nondirective, self-esteem-oriented therapy, humanistic psychologist Abraham Maslow eventually began to question the use of this approach for children. He argued that

> . . . self-actualization does not occur in young people . . . they have not learned how to be patient; nor have they learned enough about evil in themselves and others . . . nor have they generally become knowledgeable and educated enough to open the possibility of becoming wise. They have not acquired enough courage to be unpopular, to be unashamed about being openly virtuous.[14]

Nondirective therapeutic approaches used by Rogers, Abraham Maslow, and William Coulson produced a pattern of failure in schools even in the hands of these founding experts. Coulson now spends much of his efforts trying to counter the earlier teachings of these men.

One specific objection to these programs is their use of hypnotic trance induction and suggestion techniques. Psychologists believe that the constant use of trance-induced altered states of consciousness might cause difficulty for some students in differentiating reality and fantasy. An altered mental state is the mind's defense mechanism, particularly in children, for enduring extremely stressful situations. If these self-protective mechanisms are taught when a child is not under life-threatening stress, the ability to distinguish reality from fantasy in the future may be impaired.

Some people believe that affective educational programs also undermine authority. In addition to their emphasis on moral tolerance, these programs often state that there are no right or wrong answers to moral questions. This leaves students open to the considerable power of peer pressure and group conformity and reduces the validity of parental or church influence. Although this approach might leave students with an uncritically good feeling about themselves, there is little evidence that this feeling correlates to academic success or healthy, moral decisions.

Many people wonder whether schools can deal with values in a manner that isn't offensive to Christians and still be constitutional. Kilpatrick thinks that they can. He advocates "character education," an approach that fell out of favor in the 1960s.

Character education is not a method. It is a comprehensive initiation into life rather than a debate on the difficult intricacies of moral dilemmas. It assumes that most of the time we know the right thing to do; the hard part is summoning the moral will to do it. Thus its emphasis is on moral training, the process of developing good habits. Honesty, helpfulness, and self-control must become second nature or instinctive responses to life's daily temptations and difficulties.

In reality, one cannot choose to do the right thing unless he or she has the capacity to do so. Selfless behavior is possible only for those who have been trained, via modeling and correction, not to be self-centered. Until we recognize that the virtuous path is the more difficult one, we rob our children of even the possibility of moral discipline.

Values-clarification methods, on the other hand, are easy to teach and are fun for the kids. They require little commitment or moral persuasion.

The apostle Paul wrote to the church at Philippi,

> Whatever is true, whatever is honorable, whatever is right, whatever is pure, whatever is lovely, whatever is of good repute, if there is any excellence and if anything worthy of praise, let your mind dwell on these things. (Phil. 4:8 NASB)

This maxim transfers well into the secular realm. Children who are exposed to noble, virtuous behavior and who are given heroes who exhibit selfless sacrifice are much more likely to do the same when they are confronted with moral choices.

Endnotes

Chapter 1
1. Paedogus 2:10, 96, 1.
2. Ann Speckhard, "The Psycho-Social Aspects of Stress Following Abortion," Ph.D. diss., University of Minnesota.
3. Nancy Michels, *Helping Women Recover from Abortion* (Minneapolis: Bethany House, 1988), 76.
4. C. Everett Koop, "The Slide to Auschwitz," in Ronald Reagan, *Abortion and the Conscience of the Nation* (Nashville: Nelson, 1984), 45–46.

Chapter 2
1. Calvin B. DeWitt, ed., *The Environment and the Christian: What Can We Learn from the New Testament?* (Grand Rapids: Baker, 1991).
2. Further development of a Christian environmental ethic can be found in Francis Schaeffer, *Pollution and the Death of Man: A Christian View of Ecology* (Wheaton, Ill.: Tyndale, 1970).

Chapter 3
1. Ian Wilmut, et al., "Viable Offspring Derives from Fetal and Adult Mammalian Cells," *Nature* 385 (1997): 810–13.
2. Tom Siegfried, "It's Hard to See a Reason Why a Human Dolly Is Evil," *Dallas Morning News,* 3 March 1997, 9D.

Chapter 4
1. Bruce L. Shelley, *The Gospel and the American Dream* (Portland, Ore.: Multnomah, 1989), 133.
2. George Barna, *What Americans Believe* (Ventura, Calif.: Regal, 1991), 80.
3. C. S. Lewis, *Mere Christianity* (New York: Macmillan, 1970), 31.
4. William Lane Craig, *Reasonable Faith: Christian Truth and Apologetics* (Wheaton, Ill.: Crossway, 1994), 61.
5. Israel Shenker, "The Provocative Progress of a Pilgrim Polymath," *Smithsonian,* May 1993, 128.
6. Graham H. Twelftree, *Dictionary of Jesus and the Gospels* (Downers Grove, Ill.: InterVarsity, 1992), 821.
7. Viktor E. Frankl, *Man's Search for Meaning* (New York: Touchstone, 1984), 82.

8. Rich Milne, who had the discussion with the Cuban pastor, told this anecdote to me.

9. Gene A. Getz, *A Biblical Theology of Material Possessions* (Chicago: Moody, 1990), chap. 40. This chapter of Dr. Getz's book is very helpful because it breaks down biblical passages by theme.

Chapter 5

1. Jerry Adler, "Kids Growing Up Scared," *Newsweek,* 10 January 1994, 44.

2. Children's Defense Fund, cited in *Newsweek,* 10 January 1994.

3. National Committee for Prevention of Child Abuse, 1994.

4. FBI Uniform Crime Report, 1993.

5. William Bennett, *The Index of Leading Cultural Indicators* (Washington: Empower America, 1993), 2.

6. John Johnston, "Kids: Growing Up Scared," *Cincinnati Enquirer,* 20 March 1994, E01.

7. Adler, "Kids Growing Up Scared," 49.

8. Cited in "Warning from Washington," *Time,* 17 May 1982, 77.

9. James Mann, "What Is TV Doing to America?" *U.S. News and World Report,* 2 August 1982, 27.

10. Leo Bogart, "Warning: The Surgeon General Has Determined That TV Violence Is Moderately Dangerous to Your Child's Mental Health," *Public Opinion,* winter 1972–73, 504.

11. Peter Plagen, "Violence in Our Culture," *Newsweek,* 1 April 1991.

12. Ibid.

13. Mark Robichaux, "MTV Is Playing a New Riff," *Wall Street Journal,* 9 February 1993.

14. Phil Rosenthal, "MTV Is Playing with Fire," *Los Angeles Times,* 11 October 1993.

15. Stewart Powell, "What Entertainers Are Doing to Your Kids," *U.S. News and World Report,* 28 October 1985.

16. George Gerbner and Larry Gross, "The Scary World of TV's Heavy Viewer," *Psychology Today,* April 1976.

17. Ibid.

Chapter 6

1. Elizabeth Tener, "You Can Help Kids Resist Drugs and Drinking," *McCall's,* August 1984, 92.

2. "Survey Links Drugs to TV," Associated Press story, 29 June 1995.

3. Ibid.

4. "Battle Strategies: Five Fronts in a War of Attrition," *Time,* 15 September 1986, 71.

5. Ibid., 73.

6. Mark Gold, *The Good News About Drugs and Alcohol* (New York: Viliard, 1991), 245.

7. "Drug Legalization: Myths and Misconceptions," U.S. Department of Justice, Drug Enforcement Administration, Seattle, Wash., 12 May 1994, 39.

8. Ibid., 43.

9. Richard Clayton and Carl Leukefeld, "The Prevention of Drug Use Among Youth: Implications of Legalization," *Journal of Primary Prevention* 22 (spring 1994).

10. "Substance Abuse: The Nation's Number One Health Problem," (Princeton, N.J.: Institute for Health Policy, Brandeis University for the Robert Wood Foundation, October 1993), 16.

11. Peggy Mann, *Reasons to Oppose Legalizing Drugs* (Danvers: Committee of Correspondence, September 1988), 3.

12. Wayne Roques, "Decriminalizing Drugs Would Be a Disaster," *Miami Herald,* 20 January 1995.

13. J. Fagan, et al., "Delinquency and Substance Abuse Among Inner-City Students," *Journal of Drug Issues* 20, no. 3.

14. "Drug Legalization: Myths and Misconceptions," 32.

15. Don Feder, "Legalizers Plan Harvard Pot Party," *Boston Herald,* 19 May 1994.

16. William Bennett, "How Intellectuals Have Failed in the Drug War," *Human Events,* 6 January 1990, 10–11.

17. Charles Tate, "Work with Marijuana: II. Sensations," *Psychology Today,* May 1971, 41–44.

18. Alan Watts, *The Joyous Cosmology* (New York: Vintage, 1962), 18–19.

Chapter 7

1. Wally N'Dow quoted in "Do UN Conferences Threaten Your Family?" *Freedom Club Report,* August 1996, 1.

2. Habitat II conference held in Istanbul, Turkey, June 3–14, 1996.

3. Ibid.

4. Maurice Strong, quoted in Concerned Women for America's *Family Voice,* May 1996.

5. Maurice Strong, comments at the 1992 UN Earth Summit quoted in *Family Voice,* May 1996.

6. Ashley Montagu, lecture at Anaheim, California, November 9, 1970, quoted in Vince Nesbitt, *Humanistic Moral and Values Education,* N.S.W. 2066 Australia, 5.

7. Paul Brandwein, *The Social Sciences* (New York: Harcourt Brace, 1970), T10.

8. Buckminster Fuller quoted in William Bowen, *Globalism: America's Demise* (Shreveport, La.: Huntington House, 1984), 20.

9. Dr. Pierce, addressing teachers in Denver, Colorado, in 1973, quoted in "Education to Remold the Child," *Parent and Child Advocates,* Rt. 4, Watertown, Wisconsin 53094, 30.

Chapter 8

1. Linda Chavez, "Best Reform for Welfare: End It," *USA Today,* 22 June 1994, 13A.
2. Kerby Anderson, "Welfare Reform: Both Parties Pushing It Now," *Eternity,* June 1987, 27.
3. Charles Murray, *Losing Ground: American Social Policy 1950–1980* (New York: Basic Books, 1984).
4. "Working vs. Welfare," *Washington Times,* 22 March 1994.
5. Joan Dillon, "Declaring War on Welfare," *Christian American,* July–August 1994, 3.
6. Marvin Olasky, *The Tragedy of American Compassion* (Washington, D.C.: Regnery, 1992).

Chapter 9

1. Allan Bloom, *The Closing of the American Mind* (New York: Simon and Schuster, 1987), 227.
2. Ronald Nash, *The Closing of the American Heart* (Richardson, Tex.: Probe Books, 1990), 9.
3. Bloom, *Closing of the American Mind,* 25.
4. Ibid., 35.
5. Nash, *Closing of the American Heart,* 47.
6. Ibid., 46.
7. Ibid., 53.
8. Ibid.
9. William Kilpatrick, *Why Johnny Can't Tell Right from Wrong* (New York: Simon & Schuster, 1992), 31.
10. Ibid., 66.
11. Bloom, *Closing of the American Mind,* 344.
12. Nash, *Closing of the American Heart,* 28.
13. Ibid., 42.
14. Ibid., 98.

Chapter 10

1. John E. Chubb and Terry M. Moe, *Politics, Markets, and America's Schools* (Washington, D.C.: Brookings Institution, 1990), 20.
2. Deborah I. Cohen, "Streets of Despair," *Education Week,* 1 December 1993, 28.
3. William J. Bennett, *The Index of Leading Cultural Indicators* (New York: Touchstone, 1994), 90.
4. Ibid., 91.
5. Chubb and Moe, *Politics, Markets, and America's Schools,* 23.
6. "School Choice Momentum," *The Washington Times,* 3 May 1999, http://www.washtimes.com/opinion/ed1.html.
7. National Center for Policy Analysis and CEO America, *Brief Analysis* no. 266 (May 22, 1998): 1.

8. Jonathan Kozol, *Savage Inequalities* (New York: Crown Publishers, 1991), 181–205.
9. National Center for Policy Analysis and CEO America, *Brief Analysis,* 2.
10. Ibid.
11. Stephen L. Carter, *The Culture of Disbelief* (New York: Basic Books, 1993), 200.

Chapter 11
1. H. Wayne House, ed., *Schooling Choices* (Portland, Ore.: Multnomah, 1988), 90.
2. Proverbs 22:6.
3. Ecclesiastes 12:1.
4. House, *Schooling Choices,* 37.
5. Ibid., 40–43.
6. Ibid., 41.
7. Ibid., 42.
8. Ibid., 43.
9. Karl Zinsmeister, "Indicators: Special Edition on School Reform," *The American Enterprise,* July–August 1998, 18.
10. Ibid., 19.
11. Karl Zinsmeister, "Indicators: Special Edition on School Reform," *The American Enterprise,* May–June 1998, 19.
12. Karl Zinsmeister, "Indicators: Special Edition on School Reform," *The American Enterprise,* July–August 1998, 18.
13. John E. Chubb and Terry M. Moe, *Politics, Markets, and America's Schools* (Washington, D.C.: Brookings Institution, 1990), see chap. 1.
14. Douglas Wilson, *Recovering the Lost Tools of Learning* (Wheaton, Ill.: Crossway, 1991), 74.

Chapter 12
1. Arthur K. Ellis and Jeffrey T. Fouts, *Research on Educational Innovations* (Princeton, N.J.: Eye on Education, 1993).
2. Ibid., 8.

Chapter 13
1. Paul Berman, *Debating P.C.: The Controversy Over Political Correctness on College Campuses* (New York: Dell, 1992), 249.
2. Ibid., 253.
3. Ibid., 257.
4. Samuel Francis, "The Other Face of Multiculturalism," *Chronicles,* April 1998, 33.
5. Richard Rorty, *Contingency, Irony, and Solidarity* (New York: Cambridge Univ. Press, 1989), 5.
6. Os Guinness and John Seel, ed., *No God but God* (Chicago: Moody, 1992), 96.

7. John Leo, "History Standards Are Bunk," *U.S. News and World Report,* 6 February 1995, 23.
8. Ibid.
9. Ibid.
10. See Richard J. Evans, *In Defense of History* (New York: W. W. Norton, 1999).
11. Paul Cameron, *Family Research Report,* newsletter of the Family Research Institute, January–February 1993, 1.
12. Rorty, *Contingency, Irony, and Solidarity,* xv.
13. Paul Cameron, *Family Research Report,* newsletter of the Family Research Institute, April–June 1991.

Chapter 14

1. "Quality Counts," a special supplement to *Education Week* 16 (January 22, 1997): 19. The text notes that a major study concluded that 75 percent of students' achievement is the result of home and family.
2. "Achievement Gap Widening, Study Reports," *Education Week,* 4 December, 1997, 1.
3. E. D. Hirsch Jr., *The Schools We Need: And Why We Don't Have Them* (New York: Doubleday, 1996), 7.
4. Ibid., 49.
5. Ibid., 20.
6. Ibid., 21.
7. Ibid., 42.
8. Ibid., 74.
9. Ibid., 66.
10. Ibid., 69.
11. Ibid., 184.
12. Douglas Wilson, *Recovering the Lost Tools of Learning: An Approach to Distinctively Christian Education* (Wheaton, Ill.: Crossway, 1991), 91.

Chapter 15

1. William G. Spady and Kit J. Marshall, "Beyond Traditional Outcome-Based Education," *Educational Leadership,* October 1991, 67.
2. "Taking Account," *Education Week,* 17 March 1993, 10.
3. Spady and Marshall, "Beyond Traditional Outcome-Based Education," 70.
4. "Amid Controversy, Pa. Board Adopts 'Learner Outcomes,'" *Education Week,* 20 January 1993, 14.
5. "Casey Seeks Legislative Changes in Pa. Learning Goals," *Education Week,* 3 February 1993, 19.
6. "Taking Account," 12.

Chapter 16

1. Andrew M. Mecca, ed., *The Social Importance of Self-Esteem* (Los Angeles: Univ. of California Press, 1989), xv.
2. Ibid., xii
3. Lorraine Plum, *Flights of Fantasy* (Carthage, Ill.: Good Apple, 1980), 2. Emphasis added.
4. William Kilpatrick, *Why Johnny Can't Tell Right from Wrong* (New York: Simon and Schuster, 1992), 216.
5. Plum, *Flights of Fantasy,* 7.
6. John Ankerberg and Craig Branch, *Thieves of Innocence* (Eugene, Ore.: Harvest House, 1993), 70.
7. Pumsy Song Book.
8. Charles Krauthammer, "Education: Doing Bad and Feeling Good," *Time,* 5 February 1990, 78.
9. Kilpatrick, *Why Johnny Can't Tell Right from Wrong,* 46.
10. Michael Ebert, "Quest's Founder Listens to Kids," *Citizen,* 20 July 1992, 15.
11. Ibid., 2.
12. Kilpatrick, *Why Johnny Can't Tell Right from Wrong,* 47.
13. Ibid., 32.
14. Ibid., 33.

Other great books
in this series include . . .

Marriage, Family, and Sexuality
Kerby Anderson, general editor
ISBN 0-8254-2031-8

Arts, Entertainment, and Christian Values
Jerry Solomon, general editor
ISBN 0-8254-2032-6

Creation, Evolution, and Modern Science
Ray Bohlin, general editor
ISBN 0-8254-2033-4

Available at your local Christian bookstore or at

kregel
PUBLICATIONS

PO Box 2607, Grand Rapids, Michigan 49501